The
Relational Grace

THE
LAME
PRINCE

NICHOLAS E. HARRIS

Published by Ariel Ministries
Edmond, Oklahoma

Scripture quotations are from the King James Version of the Bible.

Library of Congress Card Number: 96-94446
ISBN 1-57502-227-3

Cover design by
Laura A. Alfonzo

Additional copies may be obtained by sending a check for $7.95,
plus $2.50 for shipping and handling, to the address below:

Dr. Nicholas E. Harris
Ariel Ministries
P.O. Box 3616
Edmond, OK 73083-3616

The Lame Prince may be obtained by retail outlets at special rates.
Write to the above adress for more information.

To my loving wife,
Crystal,
who stood beside me
even when I could not walk.

TABLE OF CONTENTS

PREFACE

In many respects this book, The Lame Prince, is autobiographical. I wrote this work from personal experience since I, too, am a lame prince. From a young age, I truly wanted to walk in the things of God, and I tried with all my might to do so. But, my efforts were based on human effort and not in the finished work of God. I was a very religious person, a pastor of a church. I tithed, I witnessed, I prayed regularly, and I tried to do good deeds, but something was always missing. In spite of all my efforts I could not walk.

I did not find the answer to my dilemma until 1981. The situation changed when I was given a series of taped teachings recorded by a British minister whose name is Malcolm Smith. As I listened to these tapes, the light of the revelation I now call "relational" grace began to be conceived in me. The revelation became full blown when I heard Malcolm say, "Christianity is not a religion . . . it is a relationship." The ramifications of this statement were staggering to me. It opened my mind to the whole concept of the divine/human encounter, and suddenly I found myself in a new relationship with Christ. As I experienced His presence, I found that He was becoming to me "my wisdom, my righteousness, my sanctification and my redemption" (I Corinthians 1:30).

The Lame Prince provides the basic structure of this revelation of relational grace. Needless to say, this revelation has now become the focus of my ministry and has been so for the past fifteen years. Countless lives have been completely transformed when the gravity of God's grace finally dawned upon their souls. This has always been true of the message of pure, undiluted grace. It transformed the lives of the characters that will be described in this book, and it has also changed the lives of thousands of people who have come to the Lord as a result of hearing this message I have been preaching for the past fifteen years.

One thing should be considered before progressing with this book. The material you are about to read is based on an interpretational model often called "typology," or "types and shadows." Typology is applied to a text when certain divinely orchestrated life situations are lifted from the Old Testament text and interpreted through the New Testament revelation. In other words, the New Testament is used to interpret the stories of the Old Testament. The Apostle Paul set forth the veracity of this methodology when he wrote:

"However that was not first which is spiritual, but that which is natural; and afterward that which is spiritual."
(I Corinthians 15:46)

I believe the pattern of types and shadows can be seen everywhere in the Bible. First, there was Adam, then there was Christ. Adam was the natural reality, Christ was the spiritual fulfillment, and on and on the examples go. First, there was Israel, and then there was the church. First, there was law, then there was grace. First, there was the tabernacle in the wilderness, then there was the spirit-filled believer. In my view, the central characters in <u>The Lame Prince</u> all possess typological significance, and I have attempted to unravel the meanings of the types and shadows wherever they appear.

Let me add this additional qualifier. The Biblical writers do not always provide every detail in a given story, so it is occasionally necessary to employ what might be called "an educated guess." That is why I have used the words "apparently," "perhaps," or "maybe" on several occasions. However, you can rest assured that these "guesses" have solid Biblical research behind each of them.

With these qualifications in mind, let me introduce you to the tumultuous world of Israel and the 11th Century B.C. The iron age has dawned in the Middle East. At this time, the twelve tribes of Israel were struggling to forge some type of national identity. Political rivalries were raging as potential leaders struggled to secure power bases. The nation was standing on the verge of civil war.

Two enormous characters would dominate this period. As our story begins, the dominant personality of this age was named Saul ben Kish. He was the king of Israel, but waiting in the wings, rising toward immortality, was the young shepherd warrior, David ben Jesse. The story opens with young David and Jonathan, one of the sons of Saul, making a pact of friendship.

INTRODUCTION

Since the dawn of time, persons of the male gender have engaged in a ritual activity known as a "blood brotherhood pact." This pact is initiated when the participants cut their wrists. The open wounds are then clasped together allowing the blood of the participants to be exchanged. The purpose of engaging in such a ritual has never changed. Men have always believed that such an act establishes a binding relationship which will be lifelong in its duration.

When I was only eight years of age, I entered into just such a relationship with my best friend. We cut our wrists (actually we only scratched the surface of our skins), clasped our wounds together, and bled into one another's veins, thus becoming "blood brothers" forever. As those little drops of blood mingled that day, we sensed the special nature of the act we had performed. Some inner intuition seemed to tell us that we were bound together for life.

Over the years I have found that these types of rituals have been practiced for as long as the human family has lived on the earth. In fact, I have spent many hours researching the historical background of these types of blood covenant rites. Subsequently, I have discovered that these blood brotherhood pacts are a common feature of every society and culture that has ever existed. Apparently, a need exists somewhere deep in the human soul (especially among those of the male gender), to weld itself to other men who have played a significant role in their lives. I have also discovered that of all the peoples who have ever practiced this type of ritual, one particular tribal group, a family known as the sons of Israel, stands apart from all the others. The twelve tribes of Israel based everything — their friendships, their government, their marriages, their codes of conduct, their international treaties, even their understanding of the divine — upon solid covenant commitments, most of which were sealed in blood.

Even the vocabulary of these Hebrew tribes reflects their unrelenting devotion to their covenant understandings. For example, of all the thousands of words in their language, few expressions have had more importance than the words "BERITH KARAT." "BERITH" means "a covenant" or "an agreement," while "KARAT" means "to cut." By placing these two words together, the Hebrews created a phrase which meant "to cut a covenant," or "to conclude a formal agreement with another person or party by cutting flesh and shedding blood." Without the words "BERITH KARAT" there would be no religion known as Judaism.

By divine ordinance, all of Israel's covenant activities required the shedding of blood; that was especially true under the covenant that came to be known as "the Law." It contained any number of divinely ordained rituals, all of which involved voluminous bloodletting. Over the thirteen hundred years in which this covenant was in effect, countless thousands of innocent beasts were offered as sacrifices on Israel's great brazen altar.

However, God never intended for this particular sacrificial system to be permanent. In fact, it only remained in effect until He could establish a new blood covenant, one that would prove to be far more grand and far more complete than the old covenant had been. This new covenant would require the shedding of human blood, but not just any person's blood. It would necessitate the spilling of the blood of God's own Son, Jesus of Nazareth. In fact, according to Jesus' own words, His sole purpose for coming into the world was to offer His blood as a sacrifice for sin so that men and women everywhere could be reconciled to God (John 3:16, Matthew 18:11).

The Lord Jesus Christ personally offers great insight on this new covenant in John 14 - 17. This Gospel tells us that when Jesus gathered His twelve disciples about Him at His Last Supper in Jerusalem, His purpose was to prepare these men for the awful bloodletting which they would witness the next day. In the course of the evening, He described to them the deeper meaning of the things that would happen to Him on the final day of His life on earth.

As He spoke, He explained to His followers the true purpose of the messianic mission upon which He had embarked. He told them that His Father had sent Him to this earth for the express purpose of forging an entirely new covenant relationship with the human family. He assured them that the terrible events which were about to transpire were necessary because they would open a door which would enable men everywhere to enter into this new covenant agreement which His physical death would make possible.

As Jesus described this new covenant, He spoke of it in terms of a relationship. His death, He said, would forge a new relationship that could only be described in the context of a close personal friendship. Then He said this:

"Greater love hath no man than this, that he lay down his life for his friends." (John 15:13)

The interesting thing about this statement is the fact that Jesus used the plural word "friends," or "PHILOI." This Greek word is pregnant with covenant significance. As we have seen, Jesus was aware of at least two things as He addressed His disciples that evening: 1) He knew that the blood which would be shed to establish the new covenant would be His own; 2) He knew that the covenant He was about to make would involve a vast number of people, not just one. In fact, Jesus knew that this covenant would have the potential to include the entire human race. That was why Jesus used the plural word, "friends."

We can be certain that Jesus was fully aware of the cost involved in establishing a blood covenant relationship with the entire human family. Like most other Hebrew men, Jesus fully understood the various factors involved in the forging of a blood covenant agreement. He knew, for example, that when two Hebrew men entered into a blood covenant ritual together, it required three distinct commitments on the part of the participants — a willingness to exchange personal identities, a willingness to exchange all financial assets and liabilities, and an undying willingness to accept responsibility for all the seed (or offspring) of a covenant brother. Each friend had to be willing to surrender everything he possessed to his covenant partner, including his real estate, his savings accounts, his personal power of attorney, and even his name. In retrospect, we see that Jesus of Nazareth was willing to do all of these things and even more. He has proved it again and again.

So, we can deduce that the blood covenant Jesus forged at Calvary was similar in many respects to all the other blood covenants that had ever been cut over the years. There was only one enormous exception. His covenant was multiple in design. Jesus Christ personally established this covenant so that it included the entire human race in its provisions. The Bible makes it clear that God desires for every person in this world to enter into this blood covenant with His Son. He offers to all men, everywhere, the incredible opportunity to exchange their identities for that of His only begotten Son. He will take their assets, which are nothing, and exchange them for the assets of His Son, which are everything. And He will take their liabilities, which are everything, and exchange them for His Son's liabilities, which are nothing.

The truth is, while Jesus was hanging there on the cross, He was doing far more than just dying. He was establishing a means by which ordinary people would be able to lay claim to all of heaven's incredible assets. By the sacrifice of His blood, all of heaven's benefits, and more, were made available to anyone who would choose to enter into this blood covenant relationship with Him.

If the blood covenant of Christ offered us nothing more than this access to heaven's assets, it would defy the imagination. To be offered the wealth, the health, and even the life of Christ in exchange for our poverty, sickness, and death simply defies the imagination. Yet, as incredible as this may seem, Christ freely offered all of this to us, and all He asks of us in return is to give to Him our poverty, our pain, and our death.

If you are one of those persons who find this offer difficult to accept, I understand your skepticism completely. In fact, when I first heard about this offer, I was skeptical as well. I asked myself more than once, "Why would Jesus Christ choose to share all of His enormous assets with a person like me, who has nothing to offer Him in return?" The whole thing seemed preposterous.

However, I would discover later this question has a very simple answer. Jesus was motivated to make such an unbelievable offer because of His great love. We must remember that His kind of love has always been very special. The Greeks called it, "AGAPE." I call it "the God-kind-of love." It has nothing to do with those warm, gushy emotional feelings we often associate with love. "AGAPE" knows nothing about feelings, only commitment. How one feels plays little or no role in this particular expression of love because "AGAPE" is birthed in the human will, not the human emotions.

Without a doubt, Jesus understood the great risk involved in the practice of "AGAPE" love, just as He understood the risk of a blood covenant commitment. He knew just how costly both could be, especially when a person like Him, who has everything, makes a commitment to give all He has to a person who has nothing. There is always the risk of rejection and being left with nothing. Clearly such a gamble is always present in any "AGAPE" or blood covenant relationship. However, for a true blood covenant friend, no risk seems too great and no sacrifice too dear.

An excellent example of a true blood covenant relationship can be found in the book of I Samuel in the Old Testament. Three main actors are involved in this great and revealing blood covenant drama. The actors are David ben Jesse, the future king of Israel, Jonathan ben Saul, Israel's crown prince, and Jonathan's only son, a young man with the difficult name Mephibosheth. The covenant relationship between these men provides a vivid foretaste of the great blood covenant agreement that would one day be initiated between Jesus of Nazareth and the entire human family on the hill called Golgotha.

It must be understood from the outset that this great saga involving David and Jonathan is more than just an intriguing historical story. This narrative contains two teachings which are vitally important to every Christian. For one thing, this story illustrates clearly the way in which ancient blood covenant agreements were established. For another, this story offers a vivid illustration of the way in which the benefits of the blood covenant of Christ can be appropriated, even today.

As this great story of David and Jonathan unfolds, an awesome typological drama begins to develop. David, the shepherd, eventually ascends to the throne of Israel, and becomes a type and shadow of God the Father, the King of the universe. Jonathan, the crown prince, eventually dies on a distant hill and becomes a distinct type of Christ, the Son of God. And Jonathan's son, Mephibosheth, comes to represent two separate realities: initially, he will represent the fallen human family; then, later in the drama, he will represent those once fallen human beings who have accepted redemption and who now "...dwell in the house of the Lord, forever." As the events in this saga progress, they not only tell the story of three fascinating men of old, but they tell my own personal story and, perhaps, yours as well.

I have written this book with a threefold purpose in mind: 1) to make each of us aware of our place in the great blood covenant of Christ; 2) to explain the benefits that are inherent in that covenant, and 3) to share how we fallen human beings can enjoy the blessing afforded by this great covenant arrangement.

I must caution you that the most common reaction to this incredible story of covenant love is an overwhelming sense of one's own unworthiness. If you experience this reaction, I encourage you to keep reading. By the time you complete this book you will discover that you may be totally unworthy of your place in such a covenant arrangement, but you will also discover that your unworthiness will not change the fact that you have unlimited access to the opportunity of becoming, "...an heir of God and a joint heir with Christ" (Romans 8 :17).

We will begin our examination of this blood covenant saga by focusing upon the strange but wonderful relationship which developed between these two very different types of persons, Jonathan ben Saul and David ben Jesse. This will be their story, as the book of I Samuel describes it.

1

David And Jonathan

David ben Jesse and Jonathan ben Saul are two of the most important characters of the Old Testament era. One was a prince and one was a pauper. Yet the deep love and respect these two men held for one another constitutes one of the most powerful stories of covenant love ever told. In spite of the social inequalities, the prince and the pauper made an unwavering lifetime commitment to one another by agreeing to participate in several time-honored blood covenant ritual activities together. Their actions are recorded in I Samuel 18:1-3. The text states:

"And it came to pass, when he had ceased speaking unto Saul, that the soul of Jonathan was knit with the soul of David, and Jonathan loved him as his own soul. Then Jonathan and David made a covenant, because he (Jonathan) loved him (David) as his own soul."

These three verses offer several pieces of information which contribute to a fuller understanding of the covenant Jonathan and David made. The most interesting fact is the indication that the crown prince was the one who pursued this unusual friendship. The text says twice, "Jonathan loved him (David) as his own soul...." not vice versa. The role of Jonathan as the pursuer seems particularly odd when considering the contrasting social positions of these two young men. Jonathan, the aggressor, was a person of prestige and power, while David was a person of low estate.

On more than one occasion I have tried to ponder the full scope of Jonathan's commitment to David, only to find myself asking how such a totally inequitable relationship could have ever developed. Unfortunately, the text of I Samuel never answers this question, nor does it explain how or under what circumstances these two young men first came to be acquainted. In fact, by the time this relationship is introduced in the text of I Samuel, David and Jonathan were so close that the blood covenant agreement was already in the act of being consummated.

Another omission in the text of I Samuel is its failure to offer details of the blood covenant ritual in which these two men engaged. The text is oddly silent. However, from the information that has been provided, several conclusions can be drawn. For one thing, a careful reading of the text makes it clear that the ritual activities share several common characteristics with the blood covenant rituals practiced throughout the ages of time and in all social groupings.

For example, the Hebrew text of I Samuel makes it clear that David and Jonathan initiated their ritual by cutting their wrists, probably with a dagger. That cutting of the wrists is not specifically mentioned in the King James Version of the Bible, but, in the Hebrew text the word in the phrase which is translated into English as "made" ("...then Jonathan and David made a covenant") is the word "KARAT" (to cut). So the phrase should read, "...Jonathan and David cut a covenant..." Then, by using the word "knit" or tied together in I Samuel 18:1-3, the text strongly implies that the two men bound their wounds together with a cord to facilitate the exchange of blood. The wrists seem to be the most likely place for such a binding.

The question may arise, "What was the purpose of such a ritual as this? Why would two men bleed into one another's bodies?" This story provides an answer. Men of that day performed this ritual act because they believed that by exchanging blood they exchanged their basic life forces. In other words, the exchange caused the life of one participant to come to be present in the body of the other.

The Hebrew belief concerning the nature of blood was based upon the words of Moses, who wrote, "...the life of the body is in the blood..." (Deuteronomy 14:10). Because life is found in the blood, any activity that involved an exchange of blood was thought to include the exchange of identities as well. When one person's blood entered the body of another, that person's identity entered into the body of the other as well. Obviously, there could be no closer relationship than this.

So, when the ritual activities described in I Samuel 18 were concluded, these two men believed they had taken steps that had merged their identities. In a sense Jonathan had become David, and David had become Jonathan. The crown prince had become a shepherd, and the shepherd had become a crown prince.

The meaning of this act is clarified by examining the second ritual activity in which these two men engaged. I Samuel 18:4 states:

> **"And Jonathan stripped himself of the robe that was upon him and gave it to David, and his garments, even to his sword, and to his bow, and to his girdle."**

This exchange of garments had a distinct symbolic meaning for Jonathan and David. At that time in history, a person's clothing was indicative of a person's station in life. So, whenever two men exchanged garments, it was a public demonstration of their willingness to change positions, socially and economically. Jonathan was a prince! He wore princely garments! On the other hand, by that time in his life, David was both a shepherd and a warrior. He probably wore some type of uniform, if not shepherd's rags. At any rate, the value of the garments they exchanged was certainly less than an equitable arrangement. But the ritual significance of this exchange would be even less equitable. A prince agreed to become a warrior and a warrior agreed to become a prince. Naturally, such an identity exchange would forever alter the course of the lives of two men as diverse in position as Jonathan and David.

Biblical history confirms the viability of the exchange. The son of Saul did become a great warrior! The enemies of Israel trembled at the very mention of the name Jonathan ben Saul. However, his warrior's role, which brought him such great glory, eventually cost him his life. At the foot of Mount Gilboa, after a fierce battle with the Philistines, Jonathan's life came to an end. This was the ultimate price of entering into a blood covenant with David. Jonathan had willingly taken the identity of David, and by exchanging garments with David, he had assumed the role of David. The prince in the shepherd's cloak had become the warrior, and the warrior in the royal robes had become the prince. So, in a sense, at Mount Gilboa, Jonathan took upon himself the death that David would have died had he not entered into a blood covenant. In so doing, Jonathan became a substitute for David. He died in the place of the son of Jesse.

On the other hand, the crown that should have been placed on the head of Jonathan had been handed to David. When Jonathan chose to bleed into the veins of David and then offered David his own princely garments, he was saying to David ben Jesse "The crown is yours." And it was! Because of the blood covenant, the crown then legally belonged to the son of Jesse. That is the full ritual meaning of the exchange of garments.

The text of I Samuel makes it clear that Jonathan knew exactly what he was doing when he cut his covenant with David and exchanged garments. He had not been blind to the fact that he was surrendering his crown by engaging in these ritual activities, and he never regretted the decision.

Long after the covenant had been cut, when Saul was relentlessly pursuing David, Jonathan remained loyal to his covenant commitment. For example, in I Samuel 23:13-15, the historian tells us of a time when Saul's army had succeeded in driving David and his small band of warriors into a wooded area on a mountain in the wilderness of Zeph. The text states:

"And Saul sought him every day, but God delivered him not into his hand."

Those days as a fugitive were terrible for David. Saul was relentless in his pursuit. On the occasion described in I Samuel 23, Jonathan had accompanied his father's forces into this wilderness region where the son of Jesse was hiding. In the meantime, we are not told how, Jonathan learned where his blood brother was hiding. The text says this:

"And Jonathan, Saul's son, arose and went to David into the forest, and strengthened his hand in God." (I Samuel 23:16)

Here, at great personal risk, Jonathan sought out his covenant brother so that he could minister to him. David, who was weary and exhausted both physically and spiritually, was given the solace and encouragement he needed to continue his flight. What a picture! Without regard to his personal safety, Jonathan risked his very life to edify the crushed spirit of his brother.

The words Jonathan spoke to David represent one of the great prophetic utterances of the Old Testament era. He says:

"Fear not; for the hand of Saul, my father, will not find thee. Thou shalt be king over Israel, and I shall be next unto thee; and that also Saul my father knoweth."

What a beautiful statement, Jonathan, the crown prince, says to the one time shepherd, "My crown belongs to you; I have willingly given it to you; you will be number one, and I will be number two." How strange these words sound in a world where everyone considers themselves to be number one. It seems incredible that a person would willingly take a crown from his own head and place it on the head of another, and then tell that person, "I willingly stand subordinate to you."

However, his next words are even more shocking. He tells David, "My father knows this...I have made it clear; I will not wear the crown, you will." This is the ultimate example of the New Testament quality of humility. One man takes off his crown and places it on the head of another, then stoops to minister to one whose head he had just adorned; how like Jesus Christ this is!

We are not told how long the covenant brothers stayed together in the forest, but when Jonathan ceased ministering to David, they paused to renew their convenant agreement for the second time. The text states:

"And the two made a covenant before the Lord; and David abode in the forest, and Jonathan went to his horse."

I Samuel 18:4 witnesses to the fact that Jonathan and David did more than exchange their garments. They also exchanged their weapons. In the Old Testament era, this act was also a noteworthy ritual activity. The exchanging of weapons by two men indicated an unwavering commitment on the part of the participants to protect one another to the death. By trading weapons, Jonathan and David bound themselves to just such a commitment.

In this ritual act, as in the previous exchange of garments, Jonathan again allowed himself to be placed at a distinct disadvantage. Jonathan was a king's son. He wore a sword, a scabbard, a bow, and a belt, all of which he gave to the son of Jesse. David was a shepherd. All he had to offer Jonathan was a crude leather sling which, in all likelihood, a man in Jonathan's position did not know how to use. So, the willingness of Jonathan to participate in such an inequitable exchange bears witness to his complete trust and confidence in the commitment of David to their covenant. David, he believed, would honor all of the provisions of the covenant they were making, including the protective oversight of Jonathan and his family. So weapons were exchanged.

Even then the covenant ritual activities were not completed. One other crucial covenant activity was yet to be performed The two men had to swear an oath together. Granted, the swearing of this oath is not specifically mentioned in I Samuel 18:3-4, but I Samuel 20:24-32 makes it clear that oaths were spoken. According to those several verses, both men swore that they would not limit their agreement to the two of them alone. The provisions would also include their children and their children's children, often referred to as "seed" in the Old Testament. The two men swore that as long as even one of their progeny endured on this earth, their blood covenant agreement would remain in effect. Obviously, this stipulation made their convenant virtually everlasting.

Of all the stipulations of his covenant with David, Jonathan seemed most concerned about this issue. The protection of his seed seemed to trouble Jonathan greatly. To understand this concern, one of several discussions between Jonathan and David, concerning the seed of Jonathan, should be examined. That discussion is recorded in II Samuel 20.

As the events in this chapter unfold, David had become a fugitive hiding from the vengeful King Saul. For almost a year, the son of Kish had been relentlessly pursuing young David, in an attempt to kill him. Saul was jealous of the public acclaim that the youthful warrior had received following his stunning defeat of the Philistine giant, Goliath. This growing popularity of David had deeply antagonized King Saul, so he had made a vow to eliminate the threatening presence of the son of Jesse. In the light of this threat, David had been forced to go into permanent hiding.

During this period of exile, Jonathan would occasionally slip away from his father's house to minister to the needs of his blood brother. On the occasion described in I Samuel 20:24-32, Jonathan had arranged a clandestine meeting with David in a field near the village of Gibeon, and at the scheduled time, the two friends kept their appointment. As they conversed, among other considerations, Jonathan took time to remind David of the promise he had made concerning their seed. I Samuel 20:42 states:

> **"And Jonathan said to David, go in peace, forasmuch as we have sworn, both of us in the name of the Lord, saying, the Lord is between me and thee, and between my seed and your seed, FOREVER."**

This verse makes it clear that Jonathan did not consider his blood covenant to be limited to David and himself alone, but by sacred oath it included all his future children and grandchildren as well. His concern seems natural considering the fact that Jonathan had willingly changed places with David. He now saw himself as a warrior, not as a prince. Because of the risks involved in his choice of roles, Jonathan seemed to have known his time would be limited. He also knew that if his name was to endure, his seed would have to survive to maturity. So as Jonathan stood in that field outside Gibeon, both men reaffirmed their commitments to the provision of their mutual covenant.

In fact, the text of II Samuel describes in great detail how faithfully David adhered to his obligation to the offspring of Jonathan. As the story develops, the historian demonstrates the difficulty involved in the keeping of this commitment. Jonathan would only produce one child, a son, and because of a long and bloody war between the house of Saul and the house of Jesse, David eventually lost contact with this young man. Yet, in spite of that separation, David did not forget his obligations, and when the time was right, the son of Jonathan became the unwavering object of David's full covenant commitment. The thrilling way in which David fulfills that portion of his covenant obligation to Jonathan provides the theme of the chapter to follow.

2

David And Mephibosheth

In the Biblical era, the birth of a son was the most celebrated event in the life of any Hebrew man. Every descendant of Abraham considered a male heir to be a prize beyond measure. David ben Jesse was no different. He longed to be the father of many sons, and he was destined to do just that. Among his better known offspring were such well known figures as Absolom, Amnon, Adonijah, and Solomon.

Jonathan, on the other hand, would father only one son in his relatively short lifetime. As with all things concerning the house of Saul and Jonathan, even the correct name of his son has been the source of much confusion. For example, in I Chronicles 8:33, the chronicler writes:

"...and the son of Jonathan was Meribbaal."

This designation seems odd since the text of II Samuel refers to Jonathan's only son as Mephibosheth. So which of the two names is correct? The answer to this apparent dilemma is actually quite simple. The name Meribbaal is the Chaldean interpretation of the Hebrew name Mephibosheth, which explains the seeming contradiction.

Regardless of what he is called, young Mephibosheth plays a central role in the historical record of II Samuel. His tale has lasting importance in Biblical history because he appears to have been the last surviving member of the once proud house of Saul ben Kish. What had once been a great and powerful dynasty had now been reduced to this one solitary man.

Mephibosheth is not only an important character, but his role in II Samuel is a fascinating study. As I have mentioned, at his birth he was included in the blood covenant agreement his father had cut with David. And, by the stipulations of this covenant, a portion of everything that belonged to Israel's greatest king, legally belonged to him. He was as much the son and heir of David as was Absolom, Amnon, or Solomon. In New Testament terms, he was a "joint heir" of all the wealth of his covenant father's estate.

Unfortunately, Mephibosheth did not claim his full covenant inheritance for many years. Several factors contributed to this long delay. One factor was the bloody civil war which erupted in Israel following the death of Saul and Jonathan. This seemingly endless struggle for power produced a number of devastating aftereffects, including the isolation of Mephibosheth from that which was rightfully his.

A second factor in this delay was the presence of ignorance! Apparently, very few people, including Mephibosheth, knew that Jonathan had cut a covenant with David, and that a share of everything David possessed belonged to the son of Jonathan. As a result of this covenantal ignorance, this young man, who could have been living a life of wealth and splendor from the day of his father's death, appears to have lived most of his life in poverty and squalor. What a tragic tale!

However, the tale is not all doom and gloom. The impoverished condition of Mephibosheth was not destined to last forever. A series of events would occur in Jerusalem several years after the coronation of David which would finally allow Mephibosheth to appropriate everything his father secured for him when he first bled into the veins of the son of Jesse. One of the most important elements in these series of events involves the sudden appearance of that divine quality which the Bible calls "grace," or "steadfast love." This quality can be seen at work everywhere in the story. In fact, this term, "steadfast love" ("CHESID" in Hebrew), is the hub around which this entire story turns. So, before examining the story, itself, a close examination of this term, "CHESID," should be in order.

"CHESID" represents the dominant covenantal word in the Hebrew language. "CHESID" can even be defined as convenant love. In the Old Testament era, the Hebrew people would use this word, "CHESID," when they attempted to describe the loving, patient way in which God deals with his elect. No other word better describes the full depth of divine love. In fact, most New Testament scholars consider "CHESID" to be nothing less than the New Testament concept of "AGAPE" wrapped in the lovely Old Testament garments of covenant commitment. And, nowhere else in the Bible is the concept of "CHESID" more graphically illustrated than in this awesome story of David and Mephibosheth.

When the narrative opens in II Samuel 9:1, David had finally established himself as the true king of Israel. Since his coronation seven short years before, David had made great progress in the goals he had set for himself and for his nation. For one thing, he merged the once diverse and autonomous Hebrew tribes into one truly unified nation, something even Saul ben Kish had been unable to do. It was a truly amazing achievement. For another thing, David had subdued the once impregnable city of Jerusalem, and had established it as the capitol of the newly unified state of Israel.

No other Hebrew, not even Joshua ben Nun, had been able to conquer Jerusalem.

Another noted accomplishment of those early years of the reign of David was the restoration of order and structure to the royal court of Israel, which in itself was no minor task. As a corollary to this court reform, David also seized the opportunity to totally reorganize the once corrupt priesthood of Israel. But perhaps the most important accomplishment of David's early years on the throne involved the revolutionary changes which he brought to the worship activities of the state. One of his first acts as king was to send for the Ark of the covenant which had been confined for twenty years in the house of Abinadab in the village of Kiriath-jearim. He relocated the ark in a tabernacle of skins which he erected on Mount Zion. When the ark was finally in place, the young king recruited singers and musicians to praise God, in three eight-hour shifts, twenty-four hours a day, thus offering a continual praise to God. Then, with all of these remarkable achievements completed, David paused to consider the one great commitment in his life that he had not yet kept. Across the years, David had never forgotten the promise he had made to Jonathan concerning his seed; a promise David had not kept. The text implies that this failure had been a continual source of pain to the king for a number of years.

Certainly, David could have made any number of excuses for having not kept his commitment to Jonathan. After all, the bloody civil war between his house and the house of Saul had made contact with Jonathan's family virtually impossible. This conflict had been so brutal that it not only broke fellowship between his family and the family of Saul, but it also divided the entire country into two armed camps. All the while, the new king did not know whether any of Jonathan's family had survived the devastation. But, when that awful conflict ceased, and peace came to the nation of Israel, David finally had an opportunity to fulfill the terms of his long-neglected covenant promise.

As his first step, David attempted to determine whether any of Saul's house had lived through the bloodletting. David began his quest by summoning a man named Ziba who had previously served in the administration of King Saul. David reasoned that Ziba might have maintained some lingering contact with the late king's family. When Ziba presented himself, David asked him this question:

"Is there YET any that is left of the house of Saul that I might show him kindness for Jonathan's sake." (II Samuel 9:1)

David would soon discover he had, indeed, summoned the right man. Ziba quickly answered David's question. He said:

"Jonnathan has yet a son..." (II Samuel 9:3b)

The heart of David must have leaped with joy at this news. Ancient Semites, like the Jews, believed that if a man had no progeny, his name would disappear from the earth. Had Jonathan not had a surviving son, it would have meant his end. A son of Jonathan had survived...that was good news! However, there was bad news as well!! II Samuel 9:3c records Ziba as saying:

"...(he) is lame on both his feet."

So a son of Jonathan had indeed survived the conflict, but according to Ziba he was seriously impaired. He could not walk. He was "lame on his feet." Today we have difficulty understanding the gravity of these words. A condition such as lameness has few social implications in our world, but it represented a major liability at this time in Hebrew history. Any physical deformity created a huge social impediment. Deformities were usually considered to be a judgment of God for sin. In fact, some ancient cultures considered lameness to be so repugnant that children who were born in this condition were actually killed at birth. That was never the case in Israel. All children were seen as being precious to God. However, even among God's elect, the lame were often ostracized and considered to be unwholesome.

If King David was at all appalled by the news of the condition of the son of Jonathan, he did not show it. David did not seem to care that the son of Jonathan had an infirmity. The blood of Jonathan flowed in this young man's veins, the same blood that flowed in his own veins, and nothing else really seemed to matter to David. In the eyes of the king, this crippled son of Jonathan was his covenant son, and the impaired physical condition of this young man could not change that fact.

David then asked Ziba the next logical question. "Where can I find this lame son of Jonathan?" And Ziba was prepared with an answer. He said to the king:

"Behold he is in the house of Machir, the son of Ammiel, in Lo-Debar." (II Samuel 9:4b)

The king had now been given all the information he required. He not only knew that Jonathan had fathered a son, he also knew where this son of Jonathan's could be found. Without question, David was relieved to finally be able to honor the blood covenant commitment he had made to Jonathan, and he would fulfill his obligations once and for all.

An important contextual question needs to be asked at this point! The question is, "How did Mephibosheth happen to become lame? Was this young man injured, or was he born in that condition?" II Samuel 4:4 provides an answer! It states:

"And Jonathan, Saul's son, had a son who was lame in his feet. He was five years old when tidings came of Saul and Jonathan out of Jezreel, and his nurse took him up and fled; and it came to pass, as she made haste to flee that he fell and became lame and his name was Mephibosheth." (II Samuel 4:4)

According to this verse, Mephibosheth had not been born with crippled feet. This condition resulted from a terrible accident which occurred when the boy was only five years of age. The whole horrifying story can be seen in the unusual name he bore, "Mephibosheth," which in Hebrew means "a shameful thing."

Without a doubt, Jonathan would not have given his first born son such a horrible name. No loving father would call his only son, "a shameful thing." This name must have been given to him later in his life to reflect the absolutely shameful circumstances under which this boy had lost the use of his limbs. Those circumstances were as follows: according to II Samuel 4:4, the injury occurred on that awful day when King Saul and Prince Jonathan died in battle on Mount Gilboa. When news of the death of the two great warriors reached the royal residence in Gibeon, the woman who had been assigned to care for Prince Mephibosheth panicked, a fact indicated by the words of II Samuel 4:4, "...and she fled...". Only terrified people "flee."

Her flight was predicated by three facts which she knew to be true. When she put these facts together, a state of panic arose in her mind. The first fact she knew was this: her five year old ward was the only surviving heir to the throne of Saul. That fact was true! The second fact was also true! Saul was dead, so David ben Jesse would immediately lay claim to the vacant throne of Israel. And the third and final fact was true as well. Whenever a new king came to power in those days, he usually killed every survivor of the former royal house to eliminate any threats to the new regime. By putting each of these three facts she knew together, she believed that the life of her young ward was soon to be in the gravest danger. Since these three facts were all she knew, her subsequent response was quite reasonable. Her fears were justified.

Without question, her trepidations at that moment were heightened by the fact that this woman had spent most of her life serving in the house of Saul. Therefore, anything she would have known about David would have probably come from her master's lips. If that were the case, her opinion of David must have been extremely negative, since we know that Saul was never the least bit objective in his assessment of the young man from Bethlehem. Saul had a pathological fear of David, so when he discussed David, his words were tainted by his delusions. We can assume that this maid heard many twisted, tainted discussions of Jesse's son. Saul believed that David had been plotting to be king of Israel since he was a shepherd in the hills of Judeah. He also believed that David would be willing to do absolutely "anything" to wear Israel's crown, and he must have shared this point of view with anyone who would listen. From the terrified reaction of this maid when she heard the news of Saul's death, she had not only listened to Saul, but she had believed what she had heard. A cruel man like David, who would do anything to be king, would certainly kill her ward, the last surviving heir to the throne of Israel. So this woman fled in terror with the young prince wrapped in her arms. Suddenly, she stumbled, and the child slipped from her grasp, falling heavily to the floor. The impact broke both his feet, causing him to become lame.

What a shame! What an utter shame! Especially when we consider the fact that this woman had actually fled for no reason at all. Ignorance had done its dirty work. Had this little maid known one additional fact, other than the three she knew, she would not have fled. Had this woman known that a blood covenant had been cut between David and Jonathan, she would have also known that this man from whom she fled was under a solemn obligation, not only to protect her young ward, but to accept him as being his own flesh and blood. So, by blindly fleeing from David, she did not protect this child in the least. In fact, her panic only succeeded in crippling him. What an utterly shameful thing! How tragic! But the tragedy does not even stop there; it grows even deeper!

The text seems to suggest that this maid may have fled in terror, but she did not flee at random. She had a distinct destination in mind from the onset. Apparently, she decided to take the boy to a village in Transjordan known as Lo-Debar, a place where she assumed he would be safe from David. At least this is where we find Mephibosheth when he next appears in the text of II Samuel. Why the village of Lo-Debar? For one thing it was a very isolated village, and for another thing, this maid appears to have been acquainted with a man who was loyal to Saul who lived in this hamlet. The name of this man was Machir. Ziba made this clear when he told King David:

> **"Behold, he is in the house of Machir, the son of Ammiel in Lo-Debar." (II Samuel 9:4b)**

Lo-Debar was a rather pathetic little place located ten miles south of the sea of Galilee in the hills of Gilead. The Hebrew interpretation of the name of this village adds a most interesting twist to this story. In the Hebrew language, the word Lo-Debar literally means "a dry place" and that name would prove to be true in more ways than one.

If the nurse was the one who was responsible for taking Mephibosheth to this "dry place" in Transjordan, she certainly did not do the young prince a favor. Here, in Lo-Debar, Mephibosheth fell under the care and influence of this man, Machir, who was the son of Ammiel. Since II Samuel 9:4 says that Mephibosheth lived in the house of Machir, then Machir must have been the landlord of the young prince. Like the village of Lo-Debar where he lived, the name Machir in Hebrew is also highly significant. Machir, in the most literal sense, means "a salesman." When these two Hebrew names, Lo-Debar and Machir, are placed in the same context, they tell a truly fascinating story. They tell us that this lame prince, Mephibosheth, lived in a dry place, and paid rent to a salesman. Considering the surroundings and the fact that Mephibosheth was a prince, this salesman must have "pitched a great line" to have kept Mephibosheth living in a place like Lo-Debar for all those years. One might wonder why Machir would be so determined to keep a lame man like Mephibosheth under his roof. The answer is quite simple. Mephibosheth was the last in the royal lineage of Saul ben Kish. Since thousands of people in Israel still remained loyal to Saul, especially in the remote areas like Galilee and Gillead, without question the presence of Mephibosheth in the house of Machir provided the salesman enormous political clout, especially among those who opposed David. Machir felt it was in his best political interest to keep the young prince in his house.

Here, I must admit that I have "read between the lines" of the text of II Samuel, but in many ways, the actions and attitudes I see displayed by Machir remind me of some of the ways in which Satan works. For example, I know that Satan devotes a full time effort to keeping the people of God in a condition of ignorance and blindness, and the text of II Samuel seems to suggest that this is exactly what Machir did to Mephibosheth. Everything points to the fact that Machir worked continually to keep the young prince in darkness. I believe that somehow (we are not told when or how) Machir discovered the truth about the relationship that had existed between Jonathan and David. Machir reasoned that if Mephibosheth was to suddenly discover the fact that he was a covenant heir to a royal fortune, the young prince might leave this dry place, and he would lose his political clout, as well as his meal ticket. So Machir used all of his skills as a salesman to peddle a "bill of goods" to the lame prince.

Of course, this entire scenario is only an assumption on my part, but if it did develop in the way I have suggested, then Machir must have never ceased in his attempts to poison the mind of Mephibosheth against David. His goal was to coerce Mephibosheth into hating his covenant father. He must have spent a great amount of time reminding Mephibosheth that it was this man, David ben Jesse, who had caused all the misery and poverty which he was suffering. He must have told him a thousand times that this man, David, had stolen the crown that legally belonged to him; that David now sat on a throne that he, himself, should be occupying! Machir must have also reiterated over and over again that the very presence of Mephibosheth posed a threat to the throne of David, and if David was ever given the opportunity he would eliminate him altogether. That appears, at least to me, to be the "bill of goods" which Machir constantly peddled to the impressionable young Mephibosheth.

Oddly enough, Satan attempts to peddle that same lie today. The Bible establishes that all of us who are born-again Christians are covenant heirs of God. According to Romans, we are "...heirs of God and joint heirs with Christ..." In other words, all that God has is ours! But Satan constantly tries to convince us that God does not love us at all; in fact, he tries to sell us on the idea that God hates us and is out to get us. Satan simply delights in causing Christians to believe that the pain and poverty we occasionally experience have been inflicted upon us by God; these discomforts are the judgments of God against us.

A "sales pitch" such as this can only succeed where an atmosphere of ignorance exists. It is nothing more than a demonic "bill of goods." We must remember that God is not "out to get" anyone. All of the wrath that God ever felt against sin was poured upon the head of His own Son, Jesus Christ, when He hung on the cross 2000 years ago. The anger of God was quenched when Jesus whispered, "It is finished." Since those words were spoken, God has never again been angry with anyone. From that day to this, God is angry with sin, but not with sinners.

Granted, Satan continues to operate in his role as the "god of this world" (II Corinthians 4:4). At this point in history, he legally holds the dominion that God had originally bestowed upon Father Adam. This means that Satan has been able to temporarily usurp the position of the landlord of this planet, and that is a real tragedy, because whenever and wherever Satan has usurped property, he has always created a slum. Therefore, in reality we should not refer to Satan as a landlord, but as a slumlord.

The same thing was true in the case of Machir. He, too, was a slumlord. If my presuppositions are correct, for years he was able to keep this young man, Mephibosheth, in a state of continual poverty when compared to all that could have been his. In fact, it appears that Mephibosheth remained in this dry, desolate, desert environment of Transjordan for so long that he came to believe this was the very best he could expect from life.

Such attitudes are common among people who are generationally impoverished. Sociological studies suggest that people who live in a slum for a prolonged period of time tend to develop a mentality of poverty, and once that mentality is fully developed, it becomes very hard to overcome. That is why slums so often become prisons to those who live in them.

Newsweek magazine published an interesting article in 1992 which exposed a slumlord who resembles Machir in many ways. In fact, some of the attitudes of this slumlord are used by Satan, himself. For example, the article states that those unfortunate people who rented property from this man frequently complained to authorities that he refused to repair any of his crumbling properties. This, of course, is also true of Satan. He never repairs anything! Jesus said that Satan has come to this world to "kill, steal, and destroy," not repair, restore, and recreate. That was something the two slumlords shared in common.

One day, one of the human slumlord's tenants reached the end of his rope! After years of living in one of those broken-down tenements, he decided to sue this slumlord. After hearing the case, the judge ruled that this slumlord had violated his own lease agreements, and he sentenced him to live in one of his own tenement buildings until the proper repairs had been made. Meanwhile, the judge instructed the court to allow the plaintiff in the case to move into this man's beautiful home in the suburban community of Cambridge, Massachusetts, until the repairs on his apartment had been completed.

In my opinion, the decision of this judge represents justice at its finest! The slumlord was given his rightful dues. In the same fashion, the cosmic slumlord, Satan, is going to receive his dues one day as well. The Bible tells us that a day is coming when Satan will be condemned to live in his own slum, that awful "dry place" which the Bible refers to as "hell." It is a real Lo-Debar! Until that day comes Satan continues his efforts to deceive those who choose to rent his property.

I have come to the conclusion that salesmen like Satan and Machir succeed for two reasons. First, because they can be so utterly convincing, and second, because ignorance is bliss! By reading between the lines of Mephibosheth's story, we can see that the son of Jonathan completely bought the sales pitch of his treacherous landlord. Mephibosheth never understood that David was not responsible for his present impoverished status. In fact, had he known all the facts, he would have known that Machir was the one who was really responsible for his poverty. By that I mean, if Machir was truly aware of the blood covenant agreement that existed between David and Jonathan as I have suggested, and if he refused to inform Mephibosheth about his rightful place in the covenant, then it was Machir who was responsible for Mephibosheth's status, not David. I believe that Machir did not want Mephibosheth to know the real truth of who he was because he would have lost this tenant, and this tenant was valuable to him because he knew that this young man was the only man in Israel who had the potential to unseat David as king. So Machir just kept Mephibosheth in the dark awaiting his chance.

Satan has always been the "prince of darkness," and he works night and day to keep the human family in spiritual blindness and ignorance (II Corinthians 4:4). He does not want the people of God to discover that they are heirs to all the benefits of that great covenant agreement which Jesus Christ cut 2000 years ago with the first person of the God head. He knows that if the children of God actually discover the truth of who they are in Christ, they will leave their hovels in a moment. So he employs his tactics of deception and, over the years, millions of people, perhaps billions, who could have been the legal heirs of the covenant benefits provided by the death and resurrection of the Lord Jesus Christ, have lived in spiritual poverty and weakness in a desert place. Like Mephibosheth of old, they have allowed this evil salesman to convince them that this arid existence in this waterless place is the very best they can expect from life. They have allowed Satan to keep them in ignorance and darkness. They have not understood that the blood covenant agreement cut in their behalves 2000 years ago offers them more joy, more health, and more wealth than they have ever thought possible. They are blind to this. They do not understand that through the shedding of Christ's blood, everything our great God possesses belongs to them, and they are now "...heirs of God and joint-heirs with Christ" (Romans 8:17). Through ignorance and blindness, many Christians remain in a state of spiritual lameness and poverty, day after dreary day, constantly deceived by Satan's never-ending lies.

For a number of years, Mephibosheth continued to suffer from this awful lack of knowledge. The lame prince would soon deal with a royal benefactor who fully understood how a person could be kept in a state of blindness and ignorance. David knew all about the power of the lie since he, himself, had been victimized for years by the lies and deceit of others. Some of those untruths were propagated by Mephibosheth's own grandfather, Saul. David could clearly recall the mesmerizing effect of a highly effective brainwashing technique, like that administered by Machir.

Yet, as effective as the deceit of Machir appears to have been, David knew the solution to the problem. He knew exactly how to remove the effects of such a campaign from the mind of Mephibosheth. The solution was the cultivation of a relationship between Mephibosheth and himself. David knew that if he could only develop a relationship with the son of Jonathan, the young man might begin to recognize the magnitude of the lies he had been told. This step was crucial to David. He could not honor the terms of the blood covenant with Jonathan while Mephibosheth continued to believe the vicious lies he had been told.

David made the commitment to establish a relationship with this lame young man, and the approach David would use to establish this relationship would prove to be most ingenious. Only the Holy Spirit could inspire such a concept. This approach of David's, as well as its ultimate outcome, provides the focus of the following chapter in the saga of David and Mephibosheth.

3

The Restoration Of A Prince

As David pondered the alienation that existed between Mephibosheth and himself, it became increasingly clear that the personal relationship he desired with the son of Jonathan would be an impossibility as long as the young man continued to live in the house of Machir in the village of Lo-Debar. Thus, David devised a plan of action. II Samuel 9:5 states:

"Then King David sent and fetched him (Mephibosheth) out of the house of Machir the Son of Ammiel from Lo-Debar."

According to this text, the plan was launched when David ordered his own personal envoy to journey to Lo-Debar. His instructions to his envoy were quite clear. He said, "Once you arrive in Lo-Debar, seek out Mephibosheth and invite him to return to Jerusalem with you; if he agrees to accompany you, bring him to the royal palace, immediately." The order was clear! The envoy was to extend an offer to his covenant son inviting him to come to Jerusalem and reside in his house as one of his own family.

Remember, David did not have to make this offer to fulfill his covenant obligations to Jonathan. He was not required to send an envoy, nor did he have to invite Mephibosheth to live in his home. He could have done everything he had promised Jonathan he would do without inviting Mephibosheth to Jerusalem at all. For example, he could have even sent Mephibosheth a check for his portion of the royal estate, then commissioned a group "of construction workers" to build Mephibosheth a palace in Lo-Debar, and finally dispatched a company of royal guards to offer Mephibosheth protection, but such an impersonal approach would never have established a relationship with the son of Jonathan, and David knew it. For a relationship to be developed, the king and his covenant son had to be brought together, so David decided to send his envoy to Lo-Debar with an invitation that offered Mephibosheth a place in his own home.

As to the form of this invitation, David could have chosen one of two options. He could have sent his envoy with a cold, impersonal letter which said, "Dear Mephibosheth, I know you are lame, but I must not allow your condition to interfere with my plans. I realize you cannot walk on your own, but if you can manage to make your way to Jerusalem, I will present you with some unbelievably wonderful gifts, I will even provide you with a room in the royal palace; unfortunately, you must manage on your own to get to Jerusalem. I do expect you to make an effort! With best regards, King David."

Most people, in the situation of David, would require something of this nature! They would expect Mephibosheth to prove himself to them in some way. They would demand that he show good faith by doing something on his own. But not David! He would exercise a second option. He would not demand any proof of fidelity to himself, whatsoever! Like the God he served, David was a person who was totally committed to the concept of grace." Because of his total commitment to grace, David did not ask Mephibosheth to do one thing on his own. In fact, the text of II Samuel demonstrates that David ben Jesse, the king of Israel, personally took the initiative in attempting to establish a relationship with the son of Jonathan. The truth is, David presented his gracious offer to Mephibosheth long before he did a single thing to endear himself to David, which is the very definition of grace.

When the royal messenger arrived in Lo-Debar, he went directly to the house of Machir and introduced himself to Jonathan's son. The envoy then explained the reason for his visit. He informed Mephibosheth of the royal offer, and he suggested that the young man return with him to the city of Jerusalem. He was then told how the king had made provisions so that he would be able to personally reside in the royal house as a part of the king's own family! Mephibosheth understood what this meant! He was lame, but he was not stupid! He would be a prince once again! What a moment! I would have loved to have seen the face of Mephibosheth when this offer was extended. There must have been shock, disbelief, joy, and fear all at the same time.

Every time I read this great story, I see a parallel between the experience of Mephibosheth and a well known experience of the late Harry Denman, a Methodist lay evangelist, who became one of the greatest soul-winners of this century. Denman tended to view every encounter with a stranger as an opportunity to invite that person to reside in the house of his king.

On one particular night, Denman was staying in a hotel in Memphis, Tennessee. About nine o'clock in the evening, he decided to find a "lost soul" to lead to Jesus. Denman sought out the hotel bar, a place where lost people are often known to congregate. There were no patrons in the bar when Denman entered, so he selected the bartender as his next candidate for salvation. Little did Harry Denman know that he was about to meet a modern day Mephibosheth, a man who was spiritually lame in both his feet. Denman quietly slipped onto a barstool and waited until the bartender approached. The bartender politely asked him, "Can I help you, sir?"

Denman responded, "Yes you can, young man; I desperately need your assistance. Would you please stop what you're doing right now and offer a prayer for me?"

The young man was startled. In utter disbelief, he asked Denman, "What did you say, sir?"

In a clear voice Denman responded, "Young man, my name is Harry Denman and I have a problem. I need prayer right now."

Puzzled and slightly perturbed, the bartender said, "But sir, I can't pray for you; I can't even pray for myself."

Denman asked, "Why not?"

The young man replied, "Over the years, I've strayed away from God. In fact, I've done so many wicked things in my life, that even if I were to try to pray, God wouldn't listen to me. Believe me when I tell you, mister, I really can't help you. If there was ever a man God doesn't hear, it's me! Right now I'm bound for hell!"

Well, this young man was right about his eternal destination! At that moment he was indeed bound for hell; however, a loving God was about to act! The King of Glory had dispatched his own personal envoy, Harry Denman, to visit this Lo-Debar-type tavern in Memphis, Tennessee, to offer a spiritually lame young man a personal invitation to live in a king's palace in a city called the New Jerusalem and to reside there for all eternity.

As he had done thousands of times before, Denman began to tell this man about the offer of his great king. As he shared, something wonderful began to happen. God's grace suddenly appeared in that hotel tavern, and within a few moments, a crippled prince, a most unlikely person, made the decision to accompany God's messenger to heaven's throne room. This young bartender did not know it, but he was about to become a new creation; a crown was about to be placed upon his brow, and a royal robe was about to be thrown over his shoulders.

Naturally, this young man did not deserve any of these divine gifts. Indeed, by his own confession, he deserved nothing more than to spend eternity in hell. But because of the grace of God, this sinner took his place in a wonderful covenant agreement in which he had been included some 1900 years before his birth. There in that hotel tavern, this lame young man claimed the benefits of this covenant, one of which was the guarantee of dwelling forever in the palace of the King of kings, and the Lord of lords. That night this young man was saved, and he left his Lo-Debar existence behind forever. The new Jerusalem would now be his eternal home.

The question faced by Mephibosheth as he listened to the offer of the envoy was the same question that faced that young bartender in Memphis! Would Mephibosheth accept the invitation to live in the house of a king? Considering the massive propaganda campaign to which the young man had been subjected over the years, he was probably tempted to decline the offer, but he did not. Like the bartender in Memphis, Mephibosheth did not refuse the royal invitation. In spite of all he had been told about David, in spite of the "sales pitches" he had heard, Mephibosheth chose to accompany the king's emissary on his return trip to Jerusalem. And that was all he did! He was powerless to do anything more. Remember, Mephibosheth could not even stand on his feet. With his crippled limbs, he could not walk to the envoy's chariot, nor could he climb aboard. He was powerless! The envoy had to do everything. He even had to lift Mephibosheth aboard his chariot. All the work, all the loading and lifting, had to be done by the envoy, and the envoy gladly did the work! Then with all labor completed, Mephibosheth left Lo-Debar and the house of Machir and never looked back.

This decision to leave Lo-Debar was a major turning point in the life of the son of Jonathan. His residence and all his relationships would also change. A new focus would come to his life. That focus would be the creation of a relationship with David ben Jesse. Up to this point in the story, Mephibosheth and David had been dead to one another in a relational sense. No relationship existed between the two men. That would suddenly change. What had happened in Lo-Debar altered everything. The truth is, when the envoy had told Mephibosheth about the promises of his king, the young man had chosen to believe what the envoy had said, and then he did something else, something vitally important. He then acted on what he had heard and believed. The Bible refers to such a response as "faith."

A person can believe without exercising faith, but there can be no faith without believing. Obviously, Mephibosheth believed the words the envoy had spoken, or he would not have made the decision to go to Jerusalem. But faith arose in Mephibosheth at that moment when he allowed himself to be placed aboard the chariot.

I see the relationship between the exercise of faith and simply believing every time I fly on a 747. This type of aircraft is so enormous that each time I see one the question always arises, "Can something this huge really get off the ground?" Well, in my mind I believe it can. I believe with all my heart that a 747 can actually fly. But, I do not manifest faith in the ability of a 747 to fly until I get aboard, take my seat, and fasten my seat belt. That is the point at which I act in faith upon what I believe.

That was also true in the case of Mephibosheth. He could believe with all his heart that David would deliver on what the envoy had promised to him, but faith was not manifested until he took his place on the chariot. Faith arose when he was willing to trust his very life on the reliability of all that the king had promised.

The journey from Lo-Debar to Jerusalem was not an easy one, but after a long time the two weary travelers arrived in the city of David. I can only imagine how Mephibosheth must have felt as he was carried into the royal throne room. Many thoughts must have been cascading through his mind. Remember, Mephibosheth had been taught all of his life to fear the new king of Israel, so he must have wondered if this would be the end of him. The thought must have occurred to him that David ben Jesse might have invited him to Jerusalem just to get rid of him once and for all! Surely, a sense of panic and dismay were gnawing at this young man's trembling heart.

So, what did Mephibosheth do? The text of II Samuel tells us! He did exactly what most of us would do. He fell on his face before the great man on the throne in utter contrition. He fully understood that he was at the mercy of the dreaded David ben Jesse.

However, Mephibosheth need not have feared. As he lay on his face in the royal throne room, he was about to experience the same outpouring of grace that young bartender in Memphis, Tennessee, would encounter some 2000 years later. Like that bartender, Jonathan's son would not receive what he expected from the king. The man on the throne did not rage at him or threaten him. Instead, the king simply responded to the presence of his covenant son with "CHESID," with gracious acceptance.

In II Samuel 9:7, David himself explains that source of the unmerited, unsolicited love that he so freely extended toward his covenant son. He says to Mephibosheth:

"Fear not, for I will surely show thee kindness for Jonathan thy father's sake, and I will restore thee all the land of Saul thy father and thou shalt eat bread at my table continually." (II Samuel 9:7)

As II Samuel shows again and again, the source of the almost unbelievable favor and acceptance that David directed toward Mephibosheth was the undying commitment of David to the father of this young man, Jonathan ben Saul. The personal merits of Mephibosheth counted for nothing. Had his acceptance been dependent upon his performance, the crippled man would have been in serious trouble. After all, in all likelihood, for many years Mephibosheth had lain on his pallet in the house of Machir cursing David ben Jesse for having placed him in such an awful situation. He had probably never done a thing for David other than hate him. So the astounding gifts David was about to offer him (and they were astounding) could not have possibly been the result of the past commitment of Mephibosheth to the king. Without question, the kindness that David was about to extend to Mephibosheth could only be "for the sake of Jonathan," and for no other reason. As David looked down from his throne at Mephibosheth, he could possibly see something of Jonathan in the face of Mephibosheth. Only the presence of Jonathan in the face of Mephibosheth made the lame prince acceptable to the king.

The same principle applies to God's gracious acceptance of us; neither our righteous performance, nor our lack of righteous performance, counts for anything with God. Our acceptance by Him is based solely upon the past righteous performance of the heavenly Jonathan, Jesus Christ. God looks upon you and me with favor only because He can see his Son reflected in us. That favor rests upon us even when we are spiritually and morally lame. God sees the Christ in us, not our personal inabilities, and not our lack of spiritual effectiveness.

This kind of divine acceptance, this acceptance based solely upon the righteous achievements of someone other than ourselves, is known as grace. It is grace that has the power to enable us to stand blameless before God, and it is grace that will establish our positions as the adopted "sons of God." And this grace is not limited; it is limitless. The New Testament makes this clear, again and again. Our standing before God now, and our standing at the final judgment, is and will be based solely upon what Christ has done, and His presence in us, and nothing else. No wonder this grace is the most marvelous provision that God ever extended to this fallen race of ours.

Nowhere is this concept of divine grace more clearly defined and graphically illustrated than in the actions David took toward Mephibosheth in this great story of covenant love recorded in I Samuel. David's gracious actions toward his covenant son, and their typographical significance, constitute the theme of the following chapter.

4

What's In A Name?

The text of I Samuel conclusively establishes the valuable lesson David had learned from the intimate blood covenant relationship which he enjoyed with Mephibosheth's father, Jonathan. He was more aware than anyone that at the time when they entered into this bond Jonathan had everything to lose and nothing to gain. David never forgot the fact that the son of Saul did not allow that inequality of their positions to deter him. Jonathan, who was a prince, committed himself to a blood covenant pact with a poor peasant boy, who had everything to gain by entering the relationship and nothing to lose.

Now, as the son of Jonathan knelt prostrate before him, the shoe was on the other foot. David was the man with the position, the prestige, and the power, and the son of Jonathan was the impoverished beggar with nothing at all to offer a king. Because of the power of covenant love and his own sense of commitment, David offered Mephibosheth what Jonathan had offered him. King David extended blessings to this impoverished young man in a way that was both wondrous and remarkable.

David wasted little time! Within moments of Mephibosheth's arrival in Jerusalem, he surrendered to Mephibosheth all the lands that had formerly belonged to his grandfather, Saul. And then, as if his generosity had not been extravagant enough, David went one step further. He issued a declaration! Mephibosheth would be a member of his own royal family. Who would have imagined such a thing? This lame man, who only hours before had been a nobody, now found himself to be the acknowledged son of a king. Such generosity is astounding! It is shocking!

An action like this is, of course, no less than grace at its very finest. In fact, it defines the very meaning of grace. Here we see a gracious king offering a poor lame man the opportunity to become a prince, and the king asks for nothing! David demands no commitments, no sworn allegiances from Mephibosheth. He simply reached out and placed a crown on the young man's head with no strings attached; it was all a free gift. There was only one question to answer! Would Mephibosheth be wise enough to accept what David offered? Would he accept his crown and his position as a true son of David ben Jesse?

The answer to these questions soon becomes apparent in the text of II Samuel. Mephibosheth would accept David's act of grace, but he would do so very slowly. In fact, when he first heard this generous offer, his initial response was disbelief. He simply could not believe what he had heard. It would be an understatement to say that he was completely overwhelmed by such a massive outpouring of undeserved favor. II Samuel 9:8 records his reaction:

"And he lowered himself and said, what is thy servant that thou shouldest look upon such a DEAD DOG."

The words in this verse do far more than depict the utterly contrite response of Mephibosheth to the offer of the king of Israel. This response also provides the opportunity to analyze the delicate psyche of Mephibosheth. He reveals his emotional condition, the state of his subconscious mind, in the two words he uses to describe himself.

Mephibosheth, as we have previously observed, was accustomed to hearing negative descriptions of his personhood. Every time his name was spoken it had negative connotations. Someone in Mephibosheth's past, probably Machir, had given to him that derogatory name, "Shameful Thing." And Mephibosheth had claimed it. That awful name was mild when compared to the name that Mephibosheth used to describe himself. He referred to himself as "DEAD DOG."

Now, why would Mephibosheth choose such a horrible image to describe himself? There was a reason! Mephibosheth, it seems, called himself "DEAD DOG" because that was exactly how he pictured himself. His choice of names indicated his total lack of any sense of personal self-worth. This young man saw himself as having very little, if any, significance in this world. He was just an old dead dog. This statement demonstrates that those negative, oppressive feelings of personal inadequacy and worthlessness were his constant companions in life. Obviously, he saw himself through the distorted glasses of self-degradation.

Fortunately for Mephibosheth, the great king did not share his own lowly view of himself. In the estimation of David, Mephibosheth was neither a "SHAMEFUL THING" nor a "DEAD DOG." The son of Jesse saw the son of Jonathan for what he actually was, the covenant son of a powerful head of state. He was a prince by adoption, and the word prince spells "important" in any language, even though at this point in his life, Mephibosheth did not feel important. Laying there on the palace floor on his face, he only felt like a "DEAD DOG."

David had a sensitive heart, and he immediately recognized the demoralized condition of this young man. Over the years, kings encountered hundreds of people in the same emotional state. So, having dealt with this attitude on numerous occasions, David took a most interesting approach! The king simply ignored the dead dog comment altogether. At that point, he did not make the slightest attempt to prop up the devastated image of Mephibosheth. This was a very wise approach. Had David made such an attempt at that crucial moment in their fledgling relationship, Mephibosheth would have probably misunderstood the situation altogether. Experience demonstrates that an insecure person like Mephibosheth would have misinterpreted the concern of David as an outpouring of pity, and the king would have immediately been invited to participate in a pity party. Had this been allowed to happen, a healthy relationship would have never developed. David understood that insecure people tend to relish pity parties and nothing can destroy a relationship as thoroughly as a quest for pity. Typically, insecure people relish the telling and retelling of their tales of woe, what is often called "poor me" stories. The insecure falsely assume that people who hear their stories will begin to pour pity on them, a response they interpret as acceptance, and acceptance is equated with relationship. This approach never works because relationships are not built this way; only dependencies are built on pity. Had David allowed himself to pity Mephibosheth, this extraordinary opportunity to forge a relationship with the son of his covenant brother might have been lost, transformed into one of those awful "pity parties."

"Pity parties" can be interesting. Since time immemorial, they have been some of the most ubiquitous social exercises in the world. All "pity parties" have one common characteristic. The pitiers always tend to start the party by "bad mouthing" themselves. They tell others how inept they are, how unnecessary they feel, and how abused they have been. The stories never change. Frankly, I hate pity parties, and I find myself resenting those who invite me. Pitiers are so transparent. They do not fool me! I understand the dynamics at work at their parties. Their exercises in self-reproach amount to nothing more than the most juvenile kind of psychological games and I know it. I also know that by their self-degradation and "bad mouthing," they are only attempting to provoke me and others to express our disagreement with their own negative expressions of their personhoods. Of course, if they succeed in attaining a positive response, they will experience a temporary "rush" of self-importance. The problem, however, is that good feelings never last; they are only band-aids on a cancer.

One of the tragedies of this situation is the fact that many well-meaning people blindly participate in these silly mind competitions. They fail to realize that by playing these games, they are not contributing to the strengthening of the self-image of these insecure people. In fact, by responding in pity, they only contribute to the further alienation of these insecure persons from their best selves. Pity acts like a narcotic. To the insecure, it offers a temporary euphoria, but when the drug wears away, the same old realities reappear. So these negative people spin their tales of woe again, "ad infinitum, ad nauseam," not understanding that their stories not only bore others, but they even repulse them. In time, insecure people only succeed in driving away the very people they most desire to attract, and in time, they find themselves completely friendless and alone.

I personally believe that Mephibosheth was attempting to bait just such a trap for David, but the great king was far too wise for such an obvious snare. Instead of reacting, instead of taking the bait, David ignored the self-degrading words of Mephibosheth, refusing to acknowledge the statement at all.

Our Heavenly Father responds in much the same way to the negativity of his children. When we debase ourselves, He simply does not listen to us. He will not acknowledge those "DEAD DOG" type references we so often make about ourselves. God has never seen the seed of His son as being "DEAD DOGS." He sees all of us as His blood-bought children. In His sight we are all royalty; we are princes and princesses to Him; we may be morally or spiritually lame, but we are just as important to our God as Mephibosheth was to David.

The next response of David to his covenant son was truly marvelous. As the son of Jonathan cringed before his king like a "DEAD DOG," the son of Jesse did something almost too wonderful for words. II Samuel 9:9 states:

> **"The king called to Ziba, Saul's servant and said unto him, I have given unto thy master's son all that pertained to Saul and to all his house."**

This verse reemphasizes the fact that David did not stop to scold this terrified young man who bowed before him. David simply turned to Ziba and reiterated the commitments he had made to Mephibosheth moments before. He announced for a second time that all those lands which had once belonged to King Saul would now belong to Mephibosheth. What a staggering commitment that was! Think about it! King David was returning to Mephibosheth everything that Mephibosheth had lost on that day when his nurse had fled in terror from his grandfather's house. Everything that would have been his was now his, and he had not done a single thing to deserve one acre of it. Not once had he demonstrated the least sign of loyalty to either the king or his kingdom. Not once had he expressed his commitment to David or his house. Yet, by the decree of a gracious king, he was deeded a fortune. At that moment, it must have seemed to Mephibosheth that he had been "born-again", and in a relational and material sense he had. He had been declared to be a new creation.

Perhaps, at this point, this story of covenant love should be put into some degree of perspective. By now it should be clear that this wonderful story of Mephibosheth and David constitutes a brief but poignant biography of the entire Christian experience. And all of us who have believed upon Christ realize that we are as much apart of this story as were the sons of Jonathan and Jesse.

The Genesis account helps explain the biographical similarities. There we are told that an evil landlord, lied to our ancient parents, Father Adam and Mother Eve. They were told these lies by the wicked landlord of this planet, and they believed him. As a result they both fled from God and "fell" into that awful condition known as sin. In one horrible moment, both ancient parents had their feet broken! They were now morally and spiritually crippled. They found themselves totally infected with the disease of sin.

Unfortunately, the tragedy of this original act of sin did not end with Adam and Eve. When they stumbled and fell, they did not "fall" alone; their future offspring also "fell" with them, as the Apostle Paul so graphically illustrates in Romans 5:12. There Paul writes:

"Wherefore as by one man sin entered the world, and death by sin; and so death passed upon all men (when Adam fell), for that all have sinned."

That is how the spiritual and moral feet of the human family came to be broken, and that is why we often find it so difficult to walk in the things of God. We are "fallen beings!" Our fall into sin has left us lame, and the awful taint of that original sin covers us like a shroud.

In his mercy, God was prepared for this contingency. From before the creation of the world he had designed a recovery plan. He would call it "the second birth." Only the mind of God could possibly ordain something as wonderful as this experience. He gave to the human race the opportunity to start life over again. The plan of God is a kind of drama which began to unfold on the sixth day of creation. It started when God breathed into Adam's nostrils "the breath of life," and Adam became a "living soul." These two words, "living soul," are very crucial to the experience of the new birth, and they are important because the concept of the human soul and its role has been totally misunderstood in the mind of many Christians. They do not understand that the soul of Adam, and his descendants, represents that part of the human make-up which enables human beings to be unique. In all of the created order, only the descendants of Adam have the extraordinary ability to make free choices. This ability is one of the three major functions of the human soul or mind, the others being the ability to reason and emote. In addition to giving to Adam this marvelous living soul, God also placed within him a spirit, which is actually a kind of container designed to hold the very life of God. The Scripture refers to this divine life as "ZOE" or "Eternal Life."

When God first breathed His breath into Adam, he was very nearly perfect. He only lacked one thing; the spirit container within him was empty. His soul had not yet chosen what would be the ultimate source of his life. The issue was always this; would Adam choose to direct his own life or would he allow God to direct his life, working through His divine presence in his spirit person? We might say that, at this point in his existence, the man, Adam, was neither "saved" or "lost". He was simply "innocent."

The spirit person of Adam remained in this empty condition until his soul finally made the decision to exercise its freedom of choice. Adam was offered two distinct choices. He could choose to partake of "eternal uncreated life," ("ZOE"), or he could choose to partake of "created life," which was the kind of life found in the angels of heaven, including Satan and his fallen hosts. Adam, alone, would have to decide the kind of life by which he would live.

Two trees in the midst of the Garden of Eden provided the source of Adam's choices. One tree was "the tree of life," and the other was "the tree of the knowledge of good and evil." Each of the two trees bore its own distinct fruit. God had given the fruit of "the tree of the knowledge of good and evil" the power to nourish the soul of man. Under its influence, a human soul would become a self-sufficient entity, dominated by the intellect and the emotions. It would not be dependent upon God for its source.

The fruit of the second, "the tree of life" was different. The nature of God was present in this fruit. God had implanted his own divine seed in that fruit. If Adam should choose to eat of this fruit rather than the fruit of "the tree of the knowledge of good and evil," his spirit container would be filled with the eternal life of God, and Adam would never die.

But Adam did not choose to eat from "the tree of life." He chose, instead, to eat the fruit of "the tree of the knowledge of good and evil," simply because he had believed the lies of Satan and not the words of God. And as he ate the fruit, his state of innocence suddenly came to an end. Within moments of tasting this fruit, the newly nourished soul of Adam began to expand, and it did not stop until it had devoured his unnourished spirit, blocking its access to God. As far as the relationship of his spirit to God was concerned, the spirit of Adam was now dead.

The spiritual death that this fruit inflicted upon Adam was so total that it even infected his seed. His DNA was altered. His genes and chromosomes became infected with death. As a result, we who are his descendants have all inherited the same spiritual death that came upon Adam in the Garden of Eden. That is what Paul means in Romans 5 when he states that all men "fell" with Adam. Like Adam after the fall, we have all entered this world without the life of God being present in our spirits. His life is missing from us. And we will never experience this divine life source until it has been conceived in us, a situation that does not occur until God first sends His "grace" to invade our dead, unregenerated spirits to prepare us for a new birth. The key is this: without the presence of His grace, not one could ever be saved. As Paul wrote to the Ephesians:

> **By grace are ye saved through faith, and that not of yourselves, it is the gift of God..." (Ephesians 2:8)**

I like to compare the unregenerate, or dormant human spirit to a tulip bulb. Prior to being planted in the ground, a tulip bulb has a dead and lifeless appearance; it seems to be no more than an ugly brown clod. But in spite of its dead outward appearance, the possibility of life lies hidden somewhere deep inside that seemingly dead mass. A spark of life is there waiting to be ignited. The same is true of the dormant human spirit. Even within the most under serving person, the possibility of eternal life is present. That hidden spark of divine life is what the Bible calls faith. As Paul once told the Romans:

> **"To each has been given A (not "the" as the King James version suggests) measure of faith." (Romans 12:6)**

The meaning of this verse should be obvious. The Apostle affirms that under the right circumstances, that is, when touched by grace, this God-given spark has the power to erupt into eternal life. If this "measure of faith" was not innately present within our dormant spirits, none of us could ever be saved.

In His Mercy, God has decreed that the triggering mechanism for salvation, His grace, would be universally bestowed. The Creator sovereignly ordained that every person would be confronted by His grace at least once. No human being has ever been exempted or omitted. Grace is an inescapable reality for every person who has ever lived.

There is one other divinely imposed principle regarding grace. Before the foundation of the world, God ordained that His grace would work in concert with the preaching of His Word. When these three elements, grace, the Word of God, and faith come into contact, a kind of internal combustion occurs initiating the process of salvation. This collision ignites an explosion within the once dormant spirit which allows the Word of God to do its assigned work. The epistle to the Hebrews describes the Word of God as a sharp two-edged sword whose finely honed blade severs the human spirit from its life-long entrapment in the soul (Hebrews 4:12).

With the life of God occupying its rightful place, the unencumbered spirit, for the first time, can experience unhindered access to the throne of God. The believer can "enter into heavenly places in Christ Jesus" (Ephesians 1:3), because the nature of God in Christ now replaces the old fallen Adamic nature in the life of that redeemed man or woman.

Keep in mind that from the very beginning God designed the human spirit to house His own nature. As II Peter 1:4 declares, "Whereby we are given great and precious promises: that by these ye may become partakers of the divine nature..." When His divine nature takes up residence in our spirit persons, we then become new creations. In a spiritual sense, we are "born again."

In terms of the Mephibosheth saga, the parallels are clear. The messenger sent by David to Lo-Debar offers a clear illustration of the way in which God's grace works in our lives. From His royal residence in the New Jerusalem, God commissions His Holy Spirit to deliver grace to those of us who are living in spiritual poverty, in very dry and desolate places. When that messenger of grace arrives, he makes all the benefits of God's great blood covenant agreement available to us.

Even though we are spiritually and morally crippled at the time, and we usually find this offer difficult to either believe or receive, the messenger is not deterred. He persists in extending these benefits to us, explaining that they are being kept for us in the house of the king. If we are just willing to go with him, he tells us he will personally deliver us to the king's palace. He even invites those who are seriously "lame" to go with him.

Certainly, most of us accept this gracious invitation with great fear and trepidation. And, when we finally step into the presence of our Lord for the first time, we feel overwhelmed by a sense of our own unworthiness. Some people even become catatonic with fear. That was my initial reaction when I first encountered God. I was terrified of Him. After all, I had been told all my life that He was "out to get me."

However, like most other young Christians, I found this initial state of fear to be very short-lived. After only a moment in the Lord's presence, I began to realize the magnitude of the lies that I had been told. I could immediately feel His great love for me. In all my life, I had never known such a sense of love and acceptance. This wondrous display of divine grace provoked me to cry for forgiveness because of all the terrible things that I had believed about this great God of ours. Needless to say, He had forgiven me before I even asked.

Over the years, I have also found that my own story is startlingly similar to the experiences of millions of other people in this world. The encounter with divine love proves to be so wonderful that our finite human minds find it difficult to fathom. It is truly amazing.

The Mephibosheth saga also graphically illustrates the great benefits available to those who enter into a covenant relationship with God. It involves restoration of what we have lost in Adam's fall. The covenant obligates God to restore our inheritance just as David was obligated by his covenant agreement to restore everything to Mephibosheth that he had lost as a result of his having fallen from the arms of his nanny. This restoration begins the moment we believe upon Christ. God immediately restores everything we lost in the fall of Adam when we claim our places in the great blood covenant of salvation through faith in the promises of Christ.

This covenant benefit has been scripturally guaranteed for us in I Corinthians 15:22. That text tells us that our covenant maker, the Lord Jesus Christ, is the second Adam. We might say, He is the second corporate head of the human race. When we have been born of Him, He personally redeems us from every curse that has ever been associated with Adam's fall, All the lameness that the first Adam brought upon the human family has now been eliminated in those who have become the sons of God by virtue of Christ's atoning sacrifice.

In true blood covenant fashion, Christ took upon Himself all of the brokenness of the human family, and in its place He gave to us His health, His wealth, and His life. All He asks in return is that we fully surrender our poverty, disease, and death to Him. And, like Mephibosheth of old, we will be amazed when we discover that all of the blessings of the covenant have been extended to us without any merit on our part, or without any cost to us. It is a free gift.

Every redeemed Christian knows exactly how Mephibosheth felt after having personally met King David. In an instant the lame prince could see the incredible bill of goods that he had been sold. Once he had looked into David's eyes, and once he had heard the sound of his voice, his opinion of his king radically changed. What do you suppose made the difference? I believe that it related to the fact that he had entered into a personal relationship with the man from Bethlehem. Rather than knowing what others said about David, he knew David in a personal way. They were now related.

All of us who have accepted our redemption from the curse of sin know this story by heart. Before we came into a personal loving relationship with our God, we did not understand the magnitude of the celestial salesman's lie. However, once we encounter God face-to-face, it soon becomes clear that He loves us more than we could possibly imagine. He loves us so much that He even chose to become one of us and die in our place.

If the world could just grasp the greatness of this divine love, it would totally transform this planet. Many people today are tormented by the same problems that once plagued young Mephibosheth. This world is full of people who see themselves as ugly, unloved, and unlovable, and since these people often do not know God in a personal way, they cannot find an eternal foundation for their existence. That is why they tend to see life as meaningless and empty. That is why so many of them commit senseless crimes, abuse substances, involve themselves in loveless relationships, and hate themselves in general. But such an outlook changes radically when these people discover how completely they are loved by their Creator God. Suddenly, life becomes exiting, meaningful, and filled with joy.

If you have never encountered the great love that God has for you, I have some good news for you. God's messenger, His Holy Spirit, has orders from the King of Glory to extend to you a personal invitation to come and live with Him in His house. If you are willing to go with Him, He will take you to the palace of the King of kings. And I can promise you this: when you enter His house you will find more love than you have ever known in your entire life.

5

No More Labor

As David looked down from his throne at his convenant son, he could not have missed the condition of the young man's feet. He could plainly see that Mephibosheth was unable to walk. The king clearly understood that in such a condition Mephibosheth would never be able to adequately care for the vast properties that he had just surrendered. So in II Samuel 9:9-10, David says to Ziba:

> **"I have given unto thy master's son all that pertained to Saul and to all his house. Thou, therefore, thy sons, and thy servants, shall till the land for him. And thou shalt bring in the fruits that thy master's son may have food to eat."**

Here the king expands on the grace he has already provided. Since Mephibosheth could not possibly tend to his new estates himself, the king would make provisions for him. David immediately assigned someone to do the work for Mephibosheth. Surely, the lame prince was overwhelmed once again. In all his miserable life he had never experienced such unsolicited and totally undeserved expressions of love and acceptance.

I, for one, can appreciate the thoughts that were running through the mind of Mephibosheth. At one time in my own life, a gracious offer like David extended to Mephibosheth would have seemed like a fairy tale to me, especially as it related to God. Gracious acceptance and generous gifts were not the response that I had been taught to expect from the King of Glory. As a child the church taught me there was only room in God's house for people who could walk in perfection before Him. I was told that God was "out to get" those people who could not "walk their talk." And since I was one of those people, I was convinced that God would eventually "get me," not favor me.

I can honestly affirm that I was trying as hard as I could to walk in the things of God. I really did try! But I just could not see to walk! Every time I managed to rise to my feet, I fell flat on my face. My feet were too crippled to support me. Then, like the Apostle Paul, I would cry out, "O wretched man that I am, who will deliver me from this body of death? Who will deliver me from this crippled condition?" Cry as I might, I could find no answers.

I am not suggesting that I was a "bad" person; I was not. But I thought I was! My problem was quite simple; the people I truly respected, people who seemed to know all about God and what God expected of people, told me again and again that the King required all of His children, including me, to walk uprightly, talk uprightly, and think uprightly, and anyone who failed to do so would be thrown out of God's house and his inheritance would be thrown away. So, I lived in constant fear because my crippled feet would not allow me to walk.

Many years later I came to know the real truth about my King. As I read II Samuel, I discovered that God is really like David, or even better, David was like God. When I saw in the text how David reached out in grace to the crippled son of Jonathan, I finally understood that God had been trying to reach out to me all of my life. I suddenly understood that God had never expected me, nor anyone else, to do what cannot possibly be done.

The story of David and Mephibosheth proved to me that God has accepted me just as I am. I could see that even when I had been too spiritually weak to work for Him, He had willingly made arrangements for the work that I was too lame to do to be done by those who were strong enough to do it.

Was that not the very same arrangement that David had provided for Mephibosheth? Sure it was! David knew that a man in Mephibosheth's condition could not possibly till all the ground he had been given, so the great king made other arrangements. He assigned thirty-six of Saul's former servants to labor among the various estates which now belonged to Mephibosheth. These servants were personally commissioned to care for all of his lands.

Mephibosheth would not only benefit from the actual labor of Ziba's sons, but he would also benefit from their years of experience in supervising those estates. This expertise and experience would enable these vast estates to become fruitful once again. And since Ziba's sons were instructed to bring everything these estates produced to the son of Jonathan, it stands to reason that this young man would become very wealthy in a brief period of time.

Once again, the deepest spiritual truths are revealed in this arrangement, truths which after 3000 years continue to be relevant to all of us who have been adopted into God's family. Our covenant Father and King has offered to all of us the very same benefits that David extended to Mephibosheth that day. Like David's covenant son, we are not required by our King to toil and sweat; in fact, it is forbidden. In our case, all the work that ever needs to be done was completed almost 2000 years ago. All we are asked to do is rest.

The Old Testament tells this same story again and again. In a variety of places God, the King of Glory, tries to show His people that there is no work to be done in His presence. For example, one of the major images of the Old Testament is the depiction of Israel as a nation of priests. That imagery is also carried into the New Testament. There we are told that believers in Christ are a "royal priesthood." God uses dozens of illustrations to demonstrate His priests must not be found working in His presence. One of the best of these illustrations can be found in Ezekiel 44:17-19.

Here, the great exilic prophet is shown a vision of the restored temple of God, the millennial temple which will be built by Messiah in His second advent, His return to earth as the conquering Lord. Ezekiel saw that when the priests of that restored temple come into the presence of the Lord to minister to Him behind the veil of His great throne room, they will be required to take off their priestly garments and replace them with simple linen robes. Only then will they be allowed to enter and stand before the throne of God.

Ezekiel clearly states the purpose for this requirement. The priests will wear these light linen garments so they will not sweat in God's presence. Ezekiel 44:178 states:

> **"They shall have linen bonnets upon their heads, and shall have linen breeches upon their loins; they shall not gird themselves with anything that causeth <u>sweat</u>."**

This illustrates the same profound truth we find in the resting of Mephibosheth. The prophet demonstrates that when we abide in the King's house, in His royal presence, human works count for nothing. In the King's sight they are "wood, hay, and stubble" (I Corinthians 3:12). Work produces sweat, and sweat is one of the curses that came upon the human family when Adam fell. Geneses 3:19 states, "...from the <u>sweat</u> of thy face shalt thou eat bread, till thou return to the ground; for out of it thou was taken..."

In the presence of a sinless God, there is no curse; therefore, there can be no work. There can be only praise. God is on an eternal Sabbath. All the work that ever needed to be done was completed 2000 years ago, when, in the person of Jesus of Nazareth, God said, "It is finished." And those who chose to believe on Him rest with Him from their labors.

The Epistle to the Hebrews confirms this very fact. According to that great epistle, those of us who have responded to our invitation to reside in the house of the King can now enjoy the eternal Sabbath of God. This epistle assures us that our own labor has never been required. A blood covenant agreement, not our own personal effort, guarantees our place at God's table.

Once again the actions of David witness to this truth. When the king invited Mephibosheth to sit at his table, he was well aware that the young man could not work. On his own, Mephibosheth was useless! This illustrates that David did not extend this invitation because of the ability of Mephibosheth to work for him. The reason David was so gracious to Mephibosheth was for one reason and one reason alone, "for Jonathan's sake." Jonathan, had done all the work necessary for his son to sit at the king's table when he bled into the veins of David. The work was completed when the covenant was cut.

This one final observation should now be made. The place that Mephibosheth was given at David's table was not a temporary thing. David said to Ziba:

"But Mephibosheth thy master's son shall ALWAYS eat at my table."

We should always bear in mind that whenever Mephibosheth sat down at David's table, the natural sons of David were sitting at the same table. No doubt, a few of these sons resented their father's generous attitude toward Saul's grandson. In all probability, they saw this crippled man as an heir of a dynasty that had been totally devoted to the destruction of their father's monarchy. Without question, many members of their own family had died at the hands of this lame man's relatives. Yet, in spite of all this, their father was treating this young man far better than he was treating some of them, his natural born sons and legitimate heirs.

These natural sons of David must have reasoned, and with some degree of accuracy, that this lame man at their table was undeserving of the position and benefits their father had extended to him. They must have had a difficult time comprehending this everlasting blood covenant that their father had cut before they were born. They also must have had difficulty understanding the depth of their father's commitment...that he would die before he would ever dishonor the blood covenant commitment he had made with the father of this lame man at their table.

The Apostle Paul describes a similar situation in his various epistles, but especially in the Epistle to the Romans. Paul, a rabbinical student, was aware that for many centuries the natural descendants of Abraham had referred to themselves as the "sons of God." They sat at their Lord's table and they did so by virtue of their natural birth. They were the legitimate seed of Abraham, and the inheritance bequeathed to Abraham was seen by these descendants of Abraham as belonging exclusively to them.

But then, Christ appeared and the Gospel was extended to the Gentiles. The question then became, "By what right do these non-Jews come to the table of God?" Paul was prepared with an answer. He took the position that a divine/human relationship existed which was far more important in the sight of God than natural birth. That relationship was a blood covenant relationship or what Paul described as either the "promises of God" or as the "spirit of adoption." In so doing, the apostle drew upon the imagery of legal adoption as it existed in the culture of his day.

Adoption in the first century was based upon the Roman concept known as "PATRIA POTESTUS" or "the power of the father." In Roman culture, fathers exercised total power over their households, including the power to control and dispossess their sons. In that age, as long as a father was alive, his sons never came of age. They were under his authority until the day he died. This power of the father made adoption a very difficult procedure because adoption involved being transferred from the "PATRIA POTESTUS" of one father to the "PATRIA POTESTUS" of another, and Romans did not take their "PATRIA POTESTUS" lightly. However, occasionally adoptions did occur.

The adoptive procedure required two steps. The first was a ritual known as "THE MANCIPATIO." Our English word, "emancipation," comes from this Latin word. "THE MANCIPATIO" began when the natural father sold his son by placing several coins on a copper scale. Then he would repurchase his son by taking the coins off the scale and putting them back in his purse. This ritual was repeated twice, then the natural father would place the same coins on the scale for a third time, but this time he would not take the coins back. The adopting father would then place more coins on the scale than the natural father had put there. If the natural father took the coins, the "PATRIA POTESTUS" over the son was transferred to the adopting father.

This ritual was followed by step two, what was called the "VINDI-CATIO." In this ritual, the adopting father presented to a magistrate the legal case for the transference of the adoptee. This action legally established the adoption as forever valid.

This ritual activity provided four benefits to an adopted son. In the first place, it severed any rights he had formerly enjoyed in his natural family, and it provided him all the rights of a natural son in his new family. In other words, he had a new father in the most binding sense. In the second place, he became an heir to his new father's estate. Even if the father had natural sons, his place of inheritance was equal to theirs. He was a co-heir with them. In the third place, any debts the adopted son had accrued prior to the adoption were canceled. He was considered under the law to be a new person. And finally, the adopted son was considered to be so much the son of his new father that he could not marry any natural daughters of the family. To do so was considered to be incestuous.

Can there by any question that this was exactly what happened to Mephibosheth? The covenant between David and Jonathan had placed upon him the "spirit of adoption" which Paul describes in Romans 8:14-15. The apostle tells us that all of us who are led by the Spirit of God are "the sons of God," and we have received "the spirit of adoption." When Mephibosheth made the decision to climb aboard the chariot of the envoy to Lo-Debar, (the envoy being a type of the Spirit of God), the adoption procedure began. When David gave to him a place in his own family, the adoption was finalized. And in time, Mephibosheth would look at David, and with the Apostle Paul he would declare:

"When we cry Abba! Father, it is the Spirit, himself, bearing witness with our spirit that we are true children of God (the King), and if children then heirs, heirs of God and fellow heirs with Christ provided we suffer with him in order that we may be glorified with him."

Everything that belonged to the natural sons of David now included Mephibosheth. His union to Machir, his oppressive landlord, was broken and he had come under the "PATRIA POTESTUS" of his loving covenant father. He was like a new creation. His old life and old master had no authority over him. His past was canceled with all its liabilities and debts. He was now a joint-heir of the king.

So the natural sons of David had no choice except to move aside and make room for this adopted, crippled son to sit with them at their table. And that's not all. We can also be assured that David did not allow these natural sons to look upon their adopted brother with disdain. David truly saw this lame man as his very own son. He may have been a natural son of Saul's lineage, and he may have been unable to walk, but these things did not matter to David; the covenant agreement with Jonathan covered every contingency.

Obviously, this entire episode is the story of the New Testament recorded in the Old Testament. The gospels and the epistles tell the same story. There we see how the King of Heaven has invited all who are the offspring of His blood covenant partner to sit at his table with Him. Without question, many of those may have great difficulty walking, but the King has decreed that no one, not even the angels of heaven, are allowed to look upon His lame sons with contempt. These angels may be great and powerful, but the adopted sons of God are even greater. The sons have been given access to the benefits of the blood covenant agreement that God cut with His son; angels have not. Angels may be mighty singers, but they will never be able to sing "Redemption's Song" with the adopted sons of God, which is the most important song anyone can sing. Only those who have been delivered from the curse of sin and death by the blood of a precious lamb can sing that song.

One day soon Christ will return to take His bride, the redeemed Church, from this dry place where we now dwell. He will secret us away to His celestial palace to be the honorees at the feast called the "Marriage Supper of the Lamb." When the festivities begin, we will be ushered past the greatest of the angelic hosts, to be seated as guests of honor at the Lord's table. All kinds of people will be present. Some of these guests could barely walk in the things of God in their earthly existence, but that will no longer matter! All who are present at the festivities will be there based on blood covenant, not the ability to walk.

That is the major message of the story of Mephibosheth. It constitutes a most wonderful saga, and when it comes to an end, the historian summarizes the entire account with these words:

"And all who dwelt in the house of Ziba were servants unto Mephibosheth. So Mephibosheth dwelt in Jerusalem; for he did eat regularly at the king's table. And he was lame in both his feet." (II Samuel 9:12b-13)

These words in verse 13 are most revealing. They indicate that his lame condition which had afflicted Mephibosheth for fifteen years or more, was not cured by moving into David's house; neither was it cured by dining regularly at the king's table. II Samuel 9:13 makes it clear that, "...he was (still) lame in both his feet."

Why did the anointed historian feel the need to repeat the fact of Mephibosheth's lameness? The answer seems rather obvious: by repeating Mephibosheth's condition, the historian reaffirmed that it was not the young man's "good walk" that had granted him favor with the king. I must repeat again, his standing with King David was based solely upon the blood covenant that had once been cut between this great king and his father. Nothing else entered the picture, not even the fact that he could not walk. He was always welcome at the king's table. And so are we; we are always welcome at the table of our Lord, crippled feet and all. Covenant love guarantees our place. Grace is our hope and our strength.

The question arises, of course, should we be content with being lame? Should we not strive to become ambulatory? The answer to those questions provides the theme for the next chapter.

6

The Walk

Like Mephibosheth, many of us have found it difficult to walk in the things of God. The indwelling sin in our lives keeps us in a crippled state. Yet, God in His goodness has allowed us to take our place at His table. It has never been necessary for God's children to be perfectly ambulatory before taking our rightful position in the house of God. We must only respond to the invitation. Then, after a solid residential relationship has been established, we can deal with the issue of our personal walk with God. The lame Mephibosheth provides a perfect example.

When Mephibosheth first arrived in Jerusalem, he could neither walk nor work. He did not allow his condition to prevent him from accepting the invitation of David to reside in the royal palace. He must have recognized that the covenant agreement David cut with his father required the king to open his royal residence to him. The text of II Samuel also leaves the impression that Mephibosheth fully understood that his place in the royal household was guaranteed for as long as he lived. These blessings were secured by the covenant, not by what he did or failed to do.

However, in spite of the secure position which Mephibosheth enjoyed in the royal residence, he never ceased to honor his great benefactor. The text is clear about that fact! Even though the covenant was unconditional and entitled Mephibosheth to live and act pretty much as he pleased, the young man chose to honor and respect his generous king and father by adoption throughout his life.

Why was this the case? The answer can be found in the word "relationship." Because of the relationship that developed between Mephibosheth and the king, this young man who had once hated David and blamed him for his condition, came to love him dearly. Because of the love he felt toward David, he desired, above all else, to please him in every way possible.

My personal experiences in life have helped me to understand how Mephibosheth really felt about David. At the age of four, my two sisters and I were taken from a most hellish Lo-Debar-type of existence. From our births, we were all severely neglected by our biological parents. In time, we were even given up for adoption. A wonderful family petitioned the court, asking to adopt us. Soon thereafter, the case was settled, and we moved into the home of this family; among a host of other feelings, a deep sense of appreciation began to arise in my heart for my new parents. These people had rescued me from a nightmare I had been experiencing for four long years.

At first, I did not know what to think of all the changes that were occurring in my life, and I was still a little intimidated by my new parents. As time passed, a relationship began to develop between us, and by the time I started to school two years later, I was beginning to feel deeply attached to "Mom and Dad." Soon, we became as close as any natural family.

As the years passed, my relationship with my parents became increasingly important to me. I wanted to please them in every way I could, even though achieving this goal often involved a struggle between the expectations of my parents and those of my peers. I was often torn! I longed for acceptance from my friends. Yet, at the same time, I wanted to please my mother and father, and I found that I could not always do both.

Peer pressure was especially intense. My friends tended to prove their looming adult status by drinking a beer occasionally, and by smoking cigarettes, and expected me to do so. But my parents deeply disapproved of such behavior. As a result, I was constantly forced to determine where my true loyalties lay. I can say that throughout my teenage years the commitment I made to my parents almost always took precedence over my need to belong. In spite of my desire to be "one of the gang," I refused to disappoint my father and mother. My relationship with them was so strong that I refused to do many of the things my friends were doing, no matter what it might cost.

How did I resist? The answer is simple! Whenever I was tempted to violate the values of my parents, I would simply stop and remember the name I now bore; that name was and is Harris. The judge had given this name to me at the adoption proceedings. This was the name of my new father and, as the years passed, his name began to mean more and more to me. That name represented something noble and good. It identified the best man I had ever known, a man whose life had been totally devoted to personal integrity and righteous living.

Because of the relationship that existed between this man whose name I had been given, and myself, there were certain places I would not take that name, and certain things I would not do while bearing that name. I did not avoid those places nor abstain from those things because I was intimidated by my father or because he physically restrained me from doing so; that was never the case. There were places that I would not go, and things I would not do because of the deep respect I felt for the man whose name I now bore.

I am not suggesting that I never disappointed my father; I am sure that he was displeased with my behavior on more than one occasion. But my father's undying commitment to our mutual relationship was greater than all my failures in life. He always seemed to know that even when I was disobedient, I truly desired to please him in my heart. And even though I failed him at times, he continued to bless me beyond anything I deserved.

Paul makes this same point in Romans 6:1-2. Here the apostle tells us that the love relationship we now enjoy with Christ puts to death the desire to walk in sin and disobedience. In fact, the very idea of living in sin eventually becomes totally illogical. The Apostle asks here, "Why would any of us who have experienced the love and grace of Christ ever want to be separated from Him by choosing to live in sin?" He might have asked, "Why would we want to live in a crippled condition when we do not have to do so?"

In fact, this question is the theme of Romans 2-7. Through this portion of the epistle, Paul engages in a series of legal debates with an imaginary opponent over this issue of the lingering, crippling presence of sin in the lives of the believer. Paul writes in Romans 5:20,"...where sin abounded, grace abounded even more." What a powerful statement this is! But the opponent does not accept it.

So he answers back, "Now Paul, if grace is as great as you say it is, if it will cover every sin that we have ever committed or will ever commit, let's just go on sinning. After all, according to what you teach, the more sin abounds, the more grace God pours upon the world; therefore, let's sin more and more every day so we can provoke even more grace. Why walk in the things of God at all? After all, if we have Christ in us, and God has forgiven every sin even before it is committed, then why not sin more?" The imaginary opponent then adds, "Don't you see, Paul? Grace makes sin good because it allows God to operate more fully."

Paul has an immediate answer to this argument. He literally shouts, "That's preposterous! How can we who have died to sin continue to live in it?" The apostle would never accept such an idea. Relationship, alone, makes such a position inconceivable.

Anyone who understands the teaching of Paul can see that this opponent did not comprehend the Apostle's true teachings on grace at all. In the theology of Paul, the Christian life originates with a death, a "death to sin," so those who have been redeemed from sin will not continue to sin because they are now dead to it. So, in the Pauline structure, true relationship with God kills the very desire to live in sin.

And how does this death to sin occur? Paul answers this question very succinctly. This death partly involves the ritual of water baptism. We who are baptized "...have been baptized <u>into</u> his (Christ's) death." So, as far as the Apostle is concerned, our water baptism constitutes a funeral. He writes this to the Romans:

> **"We were buried therefore with him by baptism and into his death, so that as Christ was raised from the dead by the glory of the Father, we, too, might <u>walk</u> in newness of life. For if we have been united with him in a death like his, we shall certainly be united with him in a resurrection like his." (Romans 6:4-5)**

According to these verses, we who are in a loving relationship with Christ have been united to Him in two ways: 1) in His death, and 2) in His resurrection. Both events are ritually acted out in our baptism in water. When we accept Christ's death as our own, and when we witness to its reality by being obedient in baptism, we know we are redeemed from the curse of death because the deathless life of God (resurrection life) has come to reside within us. Paul continues:

> **"We know that our <u>old self</u> was crucified with him so that the <u>sinful body</u> might be destroyed, and we might no longer be enslaved to sin. For he who has died is freed from sin." (Romans 6:6-7)**

Here Paul identifies the two culprits which work continually to keep us spiritually lame; one is the "old self," and the other is the "sinful body." The "old self," Paul argues, must be "crucified" so that the "sinful body" can be "destroyed." Naturally, this "sinful body" is not our physical anatomy. When we are saved, our physical bodies are not destroyed. No, the "sinful body" represents the fallen, sinful nature that was once present in each of us. Our "sinful body" was destroyed when this thing called the "old self" was crucified with Christ.

So, who is this "old self" we must crucify? Paul answers this question clearly! The "old self" is the person that we were before we turned to Christ. This "old self" was crucified at the very moment we chose to respond in faith to the presence of God's grace. Once we responded to God's offer, He took that "old self" and nailed that "old self" to the cross with Christ.

Remember, while Christ was dying on the cross, the penalty for sin was being paid in full. God had declared from the beginning that the penalty for sin would include two distinct and separate types of death, one physical, and the other spiritual. Physical death is the cessation of bodily function. Spiritual death is eternal separation from God. Jesus warned that of the two types of death, spiritual death is the one to be feared.

In His grace, God had a remedy for both types of death....Jesus Christ. As Christ hung on the cross, He provided the solution for our spiritual death when He took this death upon Himself. He made an arrangement whereby we can consign our "old selves" to His cross, reckoning these "old selves" to be dead with Christ so that the power of the second death can be broken in us. In other words, the penalty for sin has now been paid in full. We might say that the death of the "old self" represents our "legal death." In God's sight we are dead to the person we once were. The price Jesus paid at Calvary has set us free from this death penalty associated with sin. Since this price was paid before we were even born, we cannot possibly deserve what has been given to us; Christ, Himself, did everything that would ever have to be done, and He did so without our assistance. And here is an important addendum...the heavenly King did not wait to see if we could walk before He paid the penalty of death. He would only require that we receive the free gift that He has so graciously offered. Walking comes later!

Victory over the second type of death, physical death, came when Christ rose in victory from the grave three days later. Of course, even Christians will die physically (Hebrews 9:27), but death will not hold those who are in Christ. His resurrection has become ours regardless of our abilities or inabilities to walk.

But what about Galatians 5:24? There Paul says:

"...those who belong to Christ have crucified the flesh with its passions and desires."

With all this concentration on what Christ has done, this verse refers to something we must do. Paul tells us that we must "crucify (die to) the flesh." Does this not suggest some effort on our part? Yes, if you "rightly divide" the text of Galatians. The "flesh" of which the apostle speaks is the "sinful body" not the "old self." This death is not the death of sin in us, this is our death to the indwelling power of sin that keeps us from walking.

The death of sin belongs to our past and is unrepeatable; it must be done only once. But the death to the indwelling power of sin which resides in the "sinful body" belongs to the present and requires frequent repetition. This death is a moment by moment rejection of the appetites and lusts of the physical body. It is a constant "reckoning" of ourselves to be dead to all the hungers and desires of our physical selves so we can walk in the things of God.

When we die to the desires of the "sinful body," when we "crucify the flesh," it allows us to live a life unencumbered by sin. We might say, we begin to walk! All that we must do is "reckon" ourselves as dead to sin.

We must consider sin as crucified in us. This "crucifixion of the flesh" is our "death to sin."

In our story, Mephibosheth did just this. He died to his "old self." The pauper that Mephibosheth had become when he moved to Lo-Debar died the moment he accepted the king's gracious offer to come to Jerusalem and live in the royal palace as his own son. The impoverished side of himself was forced to remain in a state of death for as long as Mephibosheth willed to continue to maintain his relations with King David. Whether or not the pauper he had once been was to remain in a state of death depended solely upon the lame prince. Each day, Mephibosheth had to decide where he would live. He could continue to live forever in the royal palace by the king's decree. But he did have a choice. He could have returned to Lo-Debar and lived there in a hovel. It was up to him! One thing he could never do was annul the covenant agreement into which he had been born. The covenant was eternal and could never be canceled. Mephibosheth could have freely chosen to reject every benefit associated with the agreement, but he could not repudiate the covenant, itself. He did not make it; therefore, he could not terminate it.

However, Mephibosheth did not choose to repudiate the covenant or reject its benefits. The love that Mephibosheth felt for King David made such choices seem ridiculous. In his mind only a fool would want to change or terminate such a relationship as this.

The experience of Mephibosheth, as recorded in II Samuel 19, has an amazing parallel to my own personal situation as I grew into manhood. Just as I often failed to please my own father at times, on at least one occasion, Mephibosheth also deeply disappointed David. To add insult to injury, this disappointment came at a time when King David found himself in one of his greatest hours of need.

As this episode begins, we find the aging king fleeing for his life. He had been driven from his palace by his own son, the much beloved Absalom. As David fled in desperation from Jerusalem, Mephibosheth's servant, Ziba, brought some badly needed supplies to the fugitive king. When David asked Ziba why his covenant son, Mephibosheth, had not come to be with him, Ziba told the king that Mephibosheth had chosen to remain in Jerusalem. In fact, Ziba reported that he had overheard Mephibosheth saying, "Today shall the house of Israel restore me the kingdom of my Father." (II Samuel 16:3).

The statement was a gross lie, as we shall later discover, but at the time these words cut David to the quick. The thought of such ingratitude was a dagger in the heart of the old king. He must have thought to himself, "After all I have done for this man, this is the thanks I get."

However, things are not always what they seem. Later, when the rebellion of Absalom had finally been quelled, and Absalom had been killed in the woods of Ephraim, the king decided to confront his covenant son, face-to-face. He decided to ask Mephibosheth personally why he had refused to come to his assistance when he had needed help so badly. When he did, the king discovered the truth. His covenant son had never rejoiced at the misfortune of David. In fact, he had been in a deep state of despair and mourning since the day David had fled from Jerusalem. And when David asked Mephibosheth why he had not chosen to follow him into exile, the young man told David that he had been prepared to go with Ziba, but in the process Ziba had deceived him, leaving the city of Jerusalem without him.

Not knowing which man was telling the truth, Mephibosheth or Ziba, David decided to test his covenant son. He said, "I am going to give Ziba half of everything that I have given you" (II Samuel 19:20). The response of the lame covenant prince to this threat is so beautiful that it must be quoted, verbatim. In the New Revised Standard Version of the Bible, Mephibosheth says, "Let him take it all, since my lord the king has arrived home safely" (II Samuel 19:30).

Clearly, Mephibosheth considered the well-being of David and the relationship he enjoyed with this great man to be more important to him than all the material things which were now his. Over the years, David's love and acceptance had become a matter of paramount concern to him. In a very real sense, this young man had utterly and completely ceased caring about himself. This commitment of Mephibosheth to David reminds me of the commitment the Apostle Paul made to the Lord Jesus Christ. He would write in Philippians 1:21, "For me to live is Christ." Mephibosheth could say, "For me to live is David." The commitment to relationship was the same for both men.

I find one element of this story to be both astounding and refreshing. Once Mephibosheth had discovered the fact that Ziba had lied about him he did not choose to flee back to his hovel in Lo-Debar in abject terror. In all likelihood, Mephibosheth was well aware of the danger he faced as a result of Ziba's grievous falsehood. If David had chosen to believe this lie, it would have been within his power to have Mephibosheth executed. When flight seemed to be in order, Mephibosheth refused to run. He chose instead to stand his ground and to trust David's commitment to the covenant agreement he had made. Time would prove the wisdom of this decision.

A secondary issue also needs to be considered in this drama. Apart from the danger the lies of Ziba posed to Mephibosheth, David's seemingly unjust reaction to Ziba's less than candid report must be examined. This, too, represents a crucial element in the story. Consider this! When David announced his intention to give Ziba half of Mephibosheth's property, the young man could have chosen to react with bitterness and malice toward the king. Mephibosheth could have ranted and raved, while angrily attempting to defend himself. But Mephibosheth was too wise for self-defense or bitterness.

His years of residence in the royal household had taught Mephibosheth to lean upon the covenant, not upon his own devices. He was not about to allow himself to return to his former life of poverty in the arid environs of distant Lo-Debar. He had not only died to his former life, but he had died to his former self. No matter how threatening his new life might have become at times, he had learned to utterly and completely trust in the covenant and in the covenant partner of his father. There was no turning back for Mephibosheth. He may have had trouble walking, but his commitment to the covenant was unwavering.

The lesson I have learned is that even though it is often difficult to walk in the things of God, we should never continue to live in the Lo-Debar of sin. Indeed, it is impossible to live in that distant place and maintain a close personal relationship with our King at the same time. We must continue to dwell in His house if we are to maintain our relationship.

The message of the response of Mephibosheth is clear! Even though some of us find it difficult to walk in the things of God, we should never return to the Lo-Debar of sin once we have departed. Our need for a relationship with our King prevents this. We simply cannot live in some distant, arid place without damaging our relationship with our King. We must remain in His house if we are to maintain this relationship.

The truth is few people who have moved into the house of the King ever want to return to their old lives. I have found that once we have left that desolate desert place and taken our residence in the palace of our King, we immediately find that we are dead to the squalor of our former existences. The desire to continue to live in that God-forsaken place evaporates. I can assure you it happened to me just this way.

However, just taking residence in the house of the King does not resolve the issue of our lameness. We often remain crippled to some extent. Deep inside most of us know that we do not have the power to walk in our own spiritual and moral strength. In fact, we have never been able to do all the things that God expects of us. When we know that we can rely upon the covenant agreement, we no longer live in fear. We know that we are the beneficiaries of a covenant that was cut 2000 years before we were even born. By faith we choose to remain in the house of our King, believing in faith that this covenant covers all our inabilities.

So, in review, we have seen how the life of Mephibosheth was radically changed when he decided to leave Lo-Debar, how he was awarded a seat at the royal table. Again, there is never any indication in the text that Mephibosheth ever considered returning to his old waterless life in Lo-Debar once he had arrived in Jerusalem. And, after having entered into a covenant relationship with David ben Jesse, he was absolutely content with his life in the royal house, even if he was not able to walk as well as David's other sons. He knew he did not deserve or earn any of the covenant benefits he had been receiving. He did not deserve to live in the royal palace, nor did he deserve to sit at the king's table, but he did not allow that to deter him. He chose to accept and utilize these benefits anyhow.

The same can be true of us. None of us are included in God's "forever family" because we have been good enough, or because we have walked worthy of the benefits that have been made available to us. We have become a part of God's family because we have died to who we once were and because we have fully accepted our Lord's invitation to dwell with Him in His house, crippled feet and all.

Certainly, the ideal of the Christian life is to learn to walk, and even to run on our crippled feet, even to be healed of our lame condition. Nevertheless, those of us who never learn to walk can still claim our seats at the King's table, based on I John 1:9. It states:

> **"If we CONFESS our sins, he is faithful and just to forgive our sins and cleanse us from all unrighteousness."**

Once we have confessed the sins of our "old selves," God abundantly pardons us. He could not do this if the penalty for our sin had not been paid-in-full. When our "old selves" have been nailed to the cross with Christ, we can then accept God's covenant favor and friendship, not based upon what we have done, but based solely upon the provisions of Christ's own blood covenant sacrifice, which includes all of us.

According to Ephesians 1:7, "In Him (Christ), we have redemption through His blood, and the forgiveness of sin according to the riches of His grace." We owe every blessing we have to the grace that has accrued to us through the covenant that Jesus Christ cut on our behalves with God the Father. Any presentation of our own merit or worthiness to God is nothing more than wasted effort. We should remember these words which Paul wrote to the Corinthians:

> **"He (God) said unto me, My grace is sufficient for thee; my strength is made perfect in weakness." (II Corinthians 12:9)**

Even those of us who are weakened by broken feet are "made perfect in weakness" because "[His] grace is sufficient." Grace enables us to sit boldly at God's table as one of His own sons, which we are.

7

The Covenant Source

A fitting conclusion to this study of blood covenant relationship and grace is found in Hebrews 6:17-18. These verses capsulize the full meaning of a blood covenant agreement. It reads:

> **"Wherein God, willing and more abundantly to show unto the heirs of promise (that is us) the immutability of his counsel, confirmed it by an oath (covenant), that by two immutable things, in which it was impossible for God to lie, we might have a strong consolation, who have fled for refuge to lay hold upon the hope set before us."**

These verses establish the fact that God has always been determined to demonstrate His unchanging commitment to the promises He has made, and that fact will never change. He will especially keep His covenant commitments with those who have been birthed into the blood covenant that He, Himself, cut with His own son at Calvary. Hebrews 6:17-18 assures us that any promise God has made to the heirs of His covenant can never be changed, even if the feet of these heirs are crippled and they cannot walk. According to this passage, God even swore an oath (a covenant) to that effect 2000 years ago. The immutability of God makes this arrangement unchangeable.

Naturally, the inability to walk in the things of God is a hindrance to our spiritual prowess, but in one sense at least, the inability to walk on our own can be an asset to us. Experience demonstrates that those who are capable of walking in their own strength are often tempted to ignore God's will and to pursue their own agendas.

But that is usually not the case among those who are aware of their inabilities. People become spiritually strong when they come to the Lord's table in total dependence upon Him, rather than trying to stand before God based on their own self-sufficiency and self-reliance. As the Apostle Paul declared, "...for when I am weak, then am I strong" (II Corinthians 12:10).

Of course, Paul also exhorted the believers in Ephesus to "be strong" (Ephesians 6:10), but the question is, "How are believers to be strong?" Paul makes the answer to this question clear when he tells believers not to try to be strong in themselves. The strength of those of us who believe is to come from "the Lord." We are strongest when we perceive ourselves to be powerless, even dead, because then we understand that our lives are hidden with God in Christ. So, we who believe are strongest when Christ is in control of our lives. He will then provide all the strength we will ever need to overcome every situation. As Paul wrote to the terribly crippled believers in Corinth:

"But of Him are ye in Christ Jesus, who of God is made unto us wisdom and righteousness and sanctification and redemption: that, according as it is written, Ye that glorieth, let him glory in the Lord." (I Cor. 1:30-31)

Only when we have finally died to ourselves, can Christ then become for us, "...our wisdom, righteousness, sanctification, and redemption" (I Corinthians 1:30). And, when Christ becomes those things for us, He will personally enable us to walk. This divine empowerment is one of the dominant benefits of the covenant that Christ established in our behalves at Calvary 2000 years ago.

Once again, the saga of Mephibosheth offers the perfect illustration of this truth. As we have seen, Mephibosheth may have been lame in both his feet and unable to stand alone, much less walk. Yet, in spite of his limitations and inabilities, he found total and complete acceptance for which he had searched all his life in the house of David.

Remember, before Mephibosheth made the decision to leave Lo-Debar, he had lived in an impoverished and powerless state. Once he arrived in Jerusalem, his status radically changed. As he sat at David's table, the whole world could see that he was no longer poor or weak. Everyone in Israel knew that he now owned vast landed estates, complete with thirty-six servants of his own, all because of his inclusion in the covenant his father had cut with King David. No person in an objective frame of mind would consider a man with such assets to be either poor nor powerless!

These very same benefits belong to all of us who have chosen to become the covenant sons of God. Because of our relationship with our King, we are no longer impoverished, and we can never be seen as being powerless. We have become "heirs" of the One who called the universe into being by the sound of His voice, and who owns everything. So, we are all extremely powerful and exceedingly rich. Even the angels of heaven are forced to obey us when we command them to act on our behalves.

Since I was adopted as a child myself, I am personally cognizant of the rights and privileges that legally belong to adopted children. These benefits are multitudinous. For one thing, an adopted child is a legal heir to his share of his adopted father's estate. I know this first hand! When my own father died several years ago, I found that I had not been omitted from his will simply because I am an adopted son. I may have been adopted, but my share of my father's estate belonged to me just as much as if I had been his natural offspring.

The same rights and privileges apply to my position as an heir of God. Since God is neither poor, sick, defeated, nor powerless, and since I am His legal heir, the curse of poverty, sickness, defeat and powerlessness does not belong to me, either. I have at my disposal an enormous power source. Since Christ is in me, even the heavenly hosts are mine to command; if I choose to instruct them, they are obliged to obey.

Granted, I still may not be able to walk very well, not nearly as well as I would like, but believe me, I am not powerless. And I am not poor either. I have inherited so much spiritual wealth that I will never need to work again.

You may be thinking, "What about Ephesians 2:10?" Does it not say:

> **"We are His workmanship, created in Christ Jesus unto good works, which God hath before ordained that we should walk in them."**

This great verse obviously encourages us to develop the ability to walk, and to work, so we must ask ourselves what constitutes these "good works" mentioned by Paul in Ephesians 2:10. Well, Paul personally chooses to define these "good works" for us. According to the apostle, the only works that God recognizes are those which have been birthed in love. As Paul wrote to the Corinthians:

> **If I bestow all my goods to feed the poor, and if I give my body to be burned, but have not loved, it profiteth me nothing." (I Corinthians 13:13)**

The apostle declares that God accepts only those works that flow from a "relationship" with Him. Obviously, a person does not have to have the ability to walk to engage in a personal relationship. And that is also true of a relationship with God. After all, a relationship with Him does not involve our feet; it involves our hearts.

Let me explain this wonderful truth with a personal illustration. I absolutely adore my wife, Chris. We have been bound together for many years in strong cords of love. Since the day I married her, I have never been unfaithful to her, but not because of a legal document that I signed in 1979. I have remained faithful to my wife because of the love relationship that we have enjoyed since before we were ever married.

However, in spite of our deep love for another, not everything I do is pleasing to Chris. There are things that she wants me to do that I am occasionally unwilling to do. In spite of my unwillingness, Chris continues to love me, and I continue to love her. The covenant relationship that we established in 1979 is still alive.

My relationship with God is much the same. Like Mephibosheth in the house of David, I realize that I do not have the strength to walk perfectly before my King. I even have difficulty displaying His kind of love to others. Since God is in me, and God is love, then love dwells in me. This relationship enables me to stand in Him, and I have based my eternal destiny on that relationship based in God's covenant love.

Returning to the great saga of covenant love and relationship which involved David ben Jesse, Jonathan ben Saul, and young Mephibosheth ben Jonathan, we have now seen how it provides us with an awesome preview of the New Testament covenant that would be initiated in our behalves at Calvary.

For the sake of clarity, the salient portions of this covenant should be reviewed once again. It should be remembered that David did not cut his blood covenant agreement with poor, crippled Mephibosheth. Long before Mephibosheth was born, David cut covenant with his father, Jonathan. Yet, Mephibosheth was included in the benefits of this covenant agreement by virtue of simply being the product of Jonathan's seed.

These same conditions apply to our covenant relationship with God. He did not cut this eternal blood covenant with us. His holiness would not allow Him to cut a covenant with you and me. We are sinful, fallen beings who would compromise His holy character should He attempt to cut covenant with us. No, this great covenant was cut between two sinless, immutable beings according to Hebrews 6:17-18. One being was God the Father, and the other was the Lord Jesus Christ. As Hebrews 6:18 declares, our covenant was drawn up between "two IMMUTABLE things." These two "immutable beings" cut their everlasting covenant long before any of us were born.

Since this covenant making activity did not involve us in any way, it is impossible for us to contribute anything to it. We can only be included by first being born of one of the participants, and then by being adopted by the other. Once this occurs, all we are required to do is accept the unbelievable benefits of our inclusion.

Hebrews 13:20 further clarifies this point. It states:

"Now the God of peace, that brought again from the dead our Lord Jesus Christ, that great shepherd of the sheep, through the blood of the everlasting covenant make you perfect in every good work to do his will, working in you that which is well pleasing in his sight

**through Jesus Christ, to whom be glory forever and
ever. Amen."**

This verse makes it clear that it was God and His Son who entered
into this better covenant that we now call the New Testament. Christ
made the commitment to shed His blood and die for the sins of the world,
while God made the commitment to raise Him from the dead once the
covenant cutting had been completed. As we know, Christ kept His side
of the commitment, and God, in turn, has kept His.

The epistle to the Hebrews tells us that after Christ's death and resurrection, He personally delivered His own precious blood to the altar of
Heaven's Holy of Holies. In so doing, He completed all the work that
would ever need to be done to enable the entire human family to participate
in the benefits of the covenant He has cut. Since He personally finished
the work of salvation, not even the most sinful men and women are
required to labor in any way in an effort to make themselves acceptable
before God; Christ did all of this for us.

And that is only the beginning of the good news. Christ not only enables
redeemed sinners like us to become acceptable before God, He also
enables us to stand without shame in His father's presence. We may be
lame in a physical sense, or even in a moral sense, but Christ enables
each of us to stand boldly in the Father's presence. When He is in us, we
stand in a state of perfect righteousness, even when we stand before God.
Remember, when Christ is "in us," His presence makes us pleasing in
God's sight. That is the good news of the Gospel of Jesus Christ.

Once we understand our covenant standing, we suddenly become exceedingly strong in our relationship with the Lord. As a result, whenever
Satan comes against us telling us that we are not good enough to call
ourselves the children of the King, all we have to say is this: "I do not call
myself a child of God because of what I have done; I call myself a child
of the King because of a covenant in which I was included long before I was
even born, and I'm simply appropriating the benefits of that agreement."

When Satan comes to annoy me, I have learned what to do. I just tell
Satan to ask my Lord to show him the blood covenant scars in His hands.
I simply cannot tell you how effective this is. Hell's malignant emissaries
cannot stand those scars. They are flagrant reminders of their inevitable
eternal defeat.

It is then that I can say to Satan, "You wicked accuser, those scars are
proof of my place in the greatest blood covenant ever cut. That is why I
can call myself the righteousness of God, that is why I can accept every
blessing that God has provided; that is why I wear Christ's own righteous
robes and walk in His sandals; it is because of the covenant that Christ
ratified for me in His own precious blood. So be gone you foul accuser!
You have no memorial in me!"

And what is true of me is true of every blood bought son and daughter of God. As the great hymnist wrote, "My hope is built on nothing less than Jesus' blood and righteousness."

Epilogue

I have often wondered what happened to Mephibosheth after the death of David. I tend to believe that David's successor, King Solomon, honored his father's commitment to this covenant son for as long as Mephibosheth lived. He probably lived in David's house until he died.

I also believe that Mephibosheth grew to love David more as he drew nearer and nearer to his own death. He knew, as he reflected on the years he had spent in the palace of this great king, that he had lived there only because of an ugly purple scar on that king's wrist.

Undoubtedly, Mephibosheth had heard David sing the psalm, "The Lord is my shepherd, I shall not want....," many times, and he must have thought to himself, "That is the story of my own life. David has been my Lord; it is he who has fed me and clothed me and bedded me and led me. While I was in his presence I feared nothing, and I wanted for nothing. He prepared a table for me every day even though my enemies were often present at the table. He continually comforted me in my crippled condition, and he allowed me to dwell in his house all the days of my life. What a wonderful lord I have had."

If Mephibosheth had known what David's greatest son would have to say to him ten generations later, he would certainly have rejoiced. Jesus Christ would have let Mephibosheth know that he could continue to live in a palace, even after his natural death. This son of David would say to him, "...in my Father's palace are many rooms; I go to prepare a room in that palace for you, and if I go I will come again to receive you unto myself that where I am there ye may be also."

That promise did not belong to Mephibosheth alone, but to all of us who have trusted our lives and our futures to that one with the ugly purple scars on His wrists, the Lord Jesus Christ.